D0826748

STRENGTH
FOR EVERY MOMENT

AVAILABLE FROM DESTINY IMAGE PUBLISHERS

STRENGTH
FOR EVERY MOMENT

50-Day Devotional

T.D. Jakes

© Copyright 2009 – T.D. Jakes

All rights reserved. This book is protected by the copyright laws of the United States of America. This book may not be copied or reprinted for commercial gain or profit. The use of short quotations or occasional page copying for personal or group study is permitted and encouraged. Permission will be granted upon request. Unless otherwise identified, Scripture quotations are taken from the New King James Version. Copyright © 1982 by Thomas Nelson, Inc. Used by permission. All rights reserved. Scripture quotations marked NIV are taken from the HOLY BIBLE, NEW INTERNATIONAL VERSION ®, Copyright © 1973, 1978, 1984 International Bible Society. Used by permission of Zondervan. All rights reserved. Scripture quotations marked KJV are taken from the King James Version. All emphasis within Scripture is the compiler's own. Please note that Destiny Image's publishing style capitalizes certain pronouns in Scripture that refer to the Father, Son, and Holy Spirit, and may differ from some publishers' styles. Take note that the name satan and related names are not capitalized. We choose not to acknowledge him, even to the point of violating grammatical rules.

Compiled by Angela Rickabaugh Shears

DESTINY IMAGE® PUBLISHERS, INC.
P.O. Box 310, Shippensburg, PA 17257-0310

"Speaking to the Purposes of God for This Generation and for the Generations to Come."

This book and all other Destiny Image, Revival Press, MercyPlace, Fresh Bread, Destiny Image Fiction, and Treasure House books are available at Christian bookstores and distributors worldwide.

For more information on foreign distributors, call 717-532-3040.

Reach us on the Internet: www.destinyimage.com.

ISBN 10: 0-7684-3130-1
ISBN 13: 978-0-7684-3130-8

For Worldwide Distribution, Printed in the U.S.A.

10 11 / 14

CONTENTS

DAY 1
I CAN DO ALL THINGS

*I can do all things through Christ who
strengthens me* (Philippians 4:13).

ECEPTION is a trap and stronghold that ensnares
many, especially those not content with their own
present state in life. The Bible instructs us that we
must learn to be content in whatever state we find ourselves.
The apostle Paul learned that lesson well: "...*for I have
learned, in whatsoever state I am, therewith to be content*" (Phil.
4:11 KJV).

This is not to imply that we should be satisfied with
being bound by the devil or be content with complacency
and mediocrity, thus not fulfilling the call of God on our
lives. Not at all. We are to work to improve ourselves while
at the same time remaining totally dependent on God.

Self-sufficiency means to be "sufficient in oneself" and not putting your faith in God's assistance. Contentment, on the other hand, is to know with certainty and absolute firm conviction that God is able to meet your every need; Jehovah is your all-sufficiency. Contentment means that you are aware that you don't covet another person's position, property, possessions, or personality. Why? Because you know and are assured that all you presently have and all that you are today is more than enough in the hands of God. Whatever you need to do to fulfill God's purpose you can do, not in your own strength, but through the strength and power of Christ that dwells within your innermost being.

The apostle Paul said:

I know how to be abased, and I know how to abound. Everywhere and in all things I have learned both to be full and to be hungry, both to abound and to suffer need. I can do all things through Christ who strengthens me (Phil. 4:12-13).

CONSIDERATIONS

1. Like Paul, have you learned to be content in your present state in life? Why or why not? What possible ways are you being deceived into discontentment?

   _____

   _____

   _____

2. In your own words, define the difference between being content and being complacent. Are you doing all you can do to fulfill the call of God in your life?

   _____

   _____

3. List five things that you think of when you consider the word "contentment." Are those things present in your life? How can you improve your contentment level?

_____

_____

_____

_____

_____

4. Contentment means that you don't covet another person's position, property, possessions, or personality. Was there a time (or times) when you were aware of coveting another's position, property, possessions, or personality? Have you completely abandoned those thoughts and desires? Why or why not?

_____

_____

_____

5. What recent steps have you taken to fulfill God's purpose for you? What additional steps can you take today, tomorrow?

_____

_____

_____

_____

MEDITATION

I know how to be abased, and I know how to abound. Everywhere and in all things I have learned both to be full and to be hungry, both to abound and to suffer need. I can do all things through Christ who strengthens me (Philippians 4:12-13).

Do you trust Christ to give you strength to do *all* things?

Day 2
Renew Your Strength

*He gives power to the weak, and to those who have
no might He increases strength. Even the youths shall
faint and be weary, and the young men shall utterly
fall, but those who wait on the Lord shall **renew
their strength**; they shall mount up with wings like
eagles, they shall run and not be weary, they shall
walk and not faint* (Isaiah 40:29-31).

When your pity party is over and you are ready for
His help, God will say, "Don't you know? Have
you not heard Who I am—the everlasting God?
I am the Creator of the universe. I am not a child; I am not
a school boy—I am God. Who do you think you're fooling?
I'm God. I hold your breath in My hands. I created your
body. I heat your blood just hot enough to keep you alive but

not so hot that you die. Who else do you allow to control your life? If it is not Me, then who? I love you. I created you in My image. I am that I am."

What more does the Lord have to do or say to show you He loves you? Don't let satan continue to fool you into thinking that God has forsaken you.

Stop doing things that you know you don't have any business doing. Repent and confess your sins instead of spending your time pointing out the sins of everyone else. Admit that you have fallen so that your healing may begin.

CONSIDERATIONS

1. Have you hosted your own pity party lately? Did you invite others? How do you feel after the party is over? Refreshed or defeated?

   _____

   _____

   _____

2. Do you believe that God is the great "I am"? What does that title or term mean to you? Define the great "I am" in two to three sentences.

   _____

   _____

   _____

   _____

3. Think of 10 ways that the Lord helps you through each day. Write them down and thank Him for each one.

_____

_____

_____

_____

_____

4. Has satan fooled you into thinking that God has forsaken you? What can you do to keep satan from fooling you?

_____

_____

5. Most people tend to judge others but don't realize the things wrong in their own lives. The next time you start to say something about another, stop first and think about issues in your own life that need to be addressed.

MEDITATION

*He gives power to the weak, and to those who have no might He increases strength. Even the youths shall faint and be weary, and the young men shall utterly fall, but those who wait on the Lord shall **renew their strength**; they shall mount up with wings like eagles, they shall run and not be weary, they shall walk and not faint* (Isaiah 40:29-31).

How many times have you felt faint and weak, but the Lord renewed your strength and you went on to accomplish your goal?

Day 3
My Understanding
Returned

*And at the end of the time I, Nebuchadnezzar, lifted
my eyes to Heaven, and **my understanding returned**
to me; and I blessed the Most High and praised and
honored Him who lives forever.... At the same time
my reason returned to me, and for the glory of my
kingdom, my honor and splendor returned to me. My
counselors and nobles resorted to me, I was restored to
my kingdom, and excellent majesty was added to me.
Now I, Nebuchadnezzar, praise and extol and honor
the King of Heaven, all of whose works are truth,
and His ways justice. And those who walk in pride
He is able to put down* (Daniel 4:34,36-37).

Repentance was the key to Nebuchadnezzar's healing and deliverance.

To fall is bad enough, but to fall and not cry out for help, refusing to repent for your sin, is worse than the fall itself. Some people are so full of pride and consumed with their own self-sufficiency that they think, "If I can't get up myself, I won't let anyone help me."

Maybe you are ashamed to let anyone know that you have fallen because you don't want them to think less of you. Is your image so important that you're willing to continue in your pitiful fallen state? Are you so deceived that you will not acknowledge that you have sinned? Stop being so proud. After all, isn't that what caused you to fall in the first place?

Pride is dangerous because it forces you to lie needlessly in a helpless state for days—and sometimes years. If you had asked for help immediately, you could have gotten up and gone on with your life.

CONSIDERATIONS

1. *Repent* means to feel remorse, self-reproach, and to feel such regret for past conduct as to change one's mind regarding it. It also means to make a change for the better as a result of contrition for one's sins. Have you repented of conduct that you know God would not approve?

   _____

   _____

2. All are guilty of prideful thoughts and actions from time to time. Think of a time that you know pride was the root of the problem. Did you dig it out and destroy it? If not, do so soon.

   _____

   _____

3. Is it hard for you to ask others or God for help?

_____

Why? _____

_____

_____

4. After you ask God for help, how do you feel? Giving your problems to Him totally brings a peace that passes all understanding. Do you know that?

_____

_____

_____

_____

5. Going on with your life after a fall or failure actually empowers you to do greater things. What greater thing can you begin today?

_____

_____

MEDITATION

*And at the end of the time I, Nebuchadnezzar, lifted
my eyes to Heaven, and **my understanding returned**
to me; and I blessed the Most High and praised and
honored Him who lives forever…. At the same time
my reason returned to me, and for the glory of my
kingdom, my honor and splendor returned to me. My
counselors and nobles resorted to me, I was restored to
my kingdom, and excellent majesty was added to me.
Now I, Nebuchadnezzar, praise and extol and honor
the King of Heaven, all of whose works are truth,
and His ways justice. And those who walk in pride
He is able to put down* (Daniel 4:34, 36-37).

Have you lost your understanding of the Most High?
Open your ears, mind, and heart and allow your understanding
and your reasoning to welcome Him into your entire being.

Day 4
Seems Right

*There is a way that **seems right** to a man, but its end
is the way of death* (Proverbs 14:12).

Have you ever noticed the way zoo caretakers handle an injured animal? Even though the caretaker is only interested in helping, the animal does not understand. It only focuses on the pain, and because of this it will strike or even kill the very person sent to help it.

Some of you may be in this very state. People who have called themselves Christians have done hurtful things to you. You did not expect them to be the ones inflicting the pain. It seemed to hurt far worse because these people professed to love the Lord.

You may have been hurt to such an extent that you no longer trust anybody, not even God. You may not have actually said, "Lord, I don't trust You," but your actions speak louder than words. Maybe you avoid reading God's Word or refuse to allow anyone to pray for you. Do you look for other ways to help alleviate and drown the pain?

God wants to deliver you! He wants to arrest every stronghold and every demonic spirit in your life—every demonic power, every type of sorcery, every hex, every spirit of unbelief, every spirit of doubt, every spirit of pride. God wants you set free now!

CONSIDERATIONS

1. When in pain, have you ever struck out at someone who was trying to help you? Explain.

   _____

   _____

   _____

2. Have you ever been hurt by another Christian? How did this experience differ from being hurt by someone who does not confess to know Jesus as Savior? Have you forgiven all those who have hurt you?

   _____

   _____

   _____

3. How fully do you trust the Lord? Can you give Him all your pain, troubles, and challenges? Why or why not?

_____

_____

_____

4. When in pain, what steps do you take to alleviate it? Do you turn to God, His Word, friends, or spouse?

_____

_____

_____

_____

5. In your own strength you can do much to alleviate pain. But with God, you can totally destroy the root of the pain and walk victoriously into the future. Do you believe this?

_____

_____

MEDITATION

*There is a way that **seems right** to a man, but its end is the way of death* (Proverbs 14:12).

The Internet, newscasts, newspapers, radio, magazines, movies, and all of the information and entertainment that bombards our senses these days are filled with messages conflicting with the truth in the Bible. Have you been caught up in something that "seems right" but is wrong according to His Word?

DAY 5
HEAR HIS VOICE

*"Today, if you will **hear His voice**, do not harden your hearts as in the rebellion." For who, having heard, rebelled? Indeed, was it not all who came out of Egypt, led by Moses? Now with whom was He angry forty years? Was it not with those who sinned, whose corpses fell in the wilderness? And to whom did He swear that they would not enter His rest, but to those who did not obey?* (Hebrews 3:15-18)

When you do not trust in God's goodness and instead walk in unbelief, you frustrate the generous grace of God. The apostle Paul wrote, *"I do not set aside the grace of God; for if righteousness comes through the law, then Christ died in vain"* (Gal. 2:21).

I warn you, brothers and sisters, do not frustrate the grace of God as the Israelites did. The Bible says that God will not always strive with humanity. God is merciful, long-suffering, and forgiving, but that does not absolve or excuse us from yielding to the Spirit so that we may be empowered to take responsibility for our own salvation.

We are without excuse, for God has given us everything we need for eternal life and godliness. Why insist on doing things your own way? Submit to God and He will give you the power to overcome every obstacle in your life, one by one.

Religion can't help you. Trying to abide by legalistic church traditions won't help you out of your situation. The only Source guaranteed to pull you through every time you ask is God Almighty.

CONSIDERATIONS

1. When you do not trust in God's goodness and instead walk in unbelief, you frustrate the generous grace of God. Are you guilty of walking in unbelief? List the areas of your life that need to be handed over to God's generous grace.

   _____

   _____

   _____

2. The apostle Paul wrote, *"I do not set aside the grace of God; for if righteousness comes through the law, then Christ died in vain"* (Gal. 2:21). Write what this verse means to you.

   _____

   _____

3. God is forgiving, but you must yield to the Spirit to be empowered. Have you yielded to the Holy Spirit? Will you give Him access to all the shadows in your being?

_____

_____

_____

_____

4. Submitting to God gives you the power to overcome every obstacle. What is the first obstacle that you would ask God to help you overcome?

_____

_____

_____

5. Explain the difference between *religion* and a *personal relationship with God*.

_____

_____

_____

MEDITATION

*"Today, if you will **hear His voice**, do not harden
your hearts as in the rebellion." For who, having
heard, rebelled? Indeed, was it not all who came out
of Egypt, led by Moses? Now with whom was He
angry forty years? Was it not with those who sinned,
whose corpses fell in the wilderness? And to whom did
He swear that they would not enter His rest, but to
those who did not obey?* (Hebrews 3:15-18)

When was the last time you were still, quiet, relaxed,
alone, and listening to His voice?

DAY 6
YOUR HEAVENLY DEFENSE ATTORNEY

Seeing then that we have a great High Priest who has passed through the heavens, Jesus the Son of God, let us hold fast our confession. For we do not have a High Priest who cannot sympathize with our weaknesses, but was in all points tempted as we are, yet without sin. (Hebrews 4:14-15).

Jesus Christ is our constant advocate and our High Priest before God. Do not allow your situation to lock you into a spirit of delusion and complacency. Remember, the devil is trying to kill you. He wants you dead. Only the Spirit of God and the blood of Jesus stand between you and destruction. Do not let satan deceive you into thinking that no one cares or that God has not heard your cries for help.

God knows your moanings and your groanings. God knows what your tears mean when they well up in your eyes. If you call on Him, He will answer you. Trust Him. If He said He will bring you through, He will.

Quit complaining about your situation. Ask God to help you; put away your pride and just ask for help. Do not allow pride to keep you immobilized in your fallen state.

Something in you has got to cry, "Lord, help! I've fallen, and I can't get up! I don't like the way I'm living; I don't like the way I'm hurting. Something in me needs to change. Something in me needs to be broken. I need to be set free by the power of God."

CONSIDERATIONS

1. Satan wants to lock you into a spirit of delusion and complacency. Have you been deluded into thinking that you are beyond hope? That is not true. God gives hope to all who believe in Him. Reading God's Word gives you strength to overcome satan's deceptions. Read a Psalm today.

   _____

2. "Only the Spirit of God and the blood of Jesus stand between you and destruction." What does this statement mean to you? Rewrite it in two to three sentences.

   _____

   _____

   _____

3. Only God can interpret your tears, anger, sadness, and heartache. When you allow Him full access, you allow Him to console, love, and comfort. Open your heart's door for Him.

4. How many times have you complained to a friend or spouse about a situation? Instead, give it to God and He will make it right.

_____

5. How many times have you cried, "Lord, help! I've fallen, and I can't get up! I don't like the way I'm living; I don't like the way I'm hurting. Something in me needs to change. Something in me needs to be broken. I need to be set free by the power of God"?

_____

MEDITATION

Seeing then that we have a great High Priest who has passed through the heavens, Jesus the Son of God, let us hold fast our confession. For we do not have a High Priest who cannot sympathize with our weaknesses, but was in all points tempted as we are, yet without sin. (Hebrews 4:14-15).

The client's best interest is the defense attorney's top priority. Allow your heavenly Defense Attorney to defend you—He won't let you down.

DAY 7
THE LORD UPHOLDS YOU

*The steps of a good man are ordered by the Lord, and
He delights in his way. Though he fall, he shall not
be utterly cast down; for **the Lord upholds** him with
His hand* (Psalm 37:23-24).

Has something so painful and overwhelming happened to you that it has affected every area of your life? Every time you kneel to pray, does your mind go back to the fact that someone broke your heart and wounded your spirit?

Have you experienced something so personally devastating that you can't discuss it with anyone? You find it difficult to trust people, and you don't know where to turn. You may feel as if everyone is grading you and evaluating your progress, when actually you are your own harshest judge.

You know you should be further along in life, but someone or some circumstance crippled your faith. Your hopes and dreams were never fulfilled.

You know you should have finished school; you know you should have been a teacher or a musician by now. By society's standards, you should already be married and have children.

Maybe you think your ministry should be further along or that you should have a successful career at this point in your life. Your dreams and goals should have been fulfilled years ago, but you've been crippled. Don't give up. There is hope for you and healing for past hurts.

God has a way of bringing us out of bondage and then making us remember where we came from. When we, like Joseph, begin to experience success and victory, God will remind us that He opened the door of the prison. He set us free.

CONSIDERATIONS

1. Has something so painful and overwhelming happened to you that it has affected every area of your life? Write about it.

   _____

   _____

   _____

   _____

2. Every time you kneel to pray, does your mind go back to the fact that someone broke your heart and wounded your spirit? Write about it.

   _____

   _____

   _____

3. Have you experienced something so personally devastating that you can't discuss it with anyone? Write about it.

_____

_____

_____

_____

4. God will bring you out of bondage and will soften the memories so you can live with them in peace. Write why you believe this truth and then trust God to make it so.

_____

_____

_____

_____

5. When you experience success and victory, God will remind you that He opened the door of the prison and set you free. Thank Him.

MEDITATION

*The steps of a good man are ordered by the Lord, and
He delights in his way. Though he fall, he shall not
be utterly cast down; for **the Lord upholds** him with
His hand* (Psalm 37:23-24).

Many have fallen because of drugs, lust, greed, false religion, and other worldly temptations; when they ask God for
help, He gently lifts them up with His hand.

DAY 8
YOUR ADVERSARY, THE DEVIL

*Be sober, be vigilant; because **your adversary the devil** walks about like a roaring lion, seeking whom he may devour* (1 Peter 5:8).

The devil is a liar! It does not matter what you have done. It does not matter where you have been. God is a God of second chances. He is the God of new beginnings. When you're down, He'll pick you up again.

When God restores you, it does not matter who is trying to bind you or who is fighting against you. All you need to know is that when God brings you up, no demon in hell can bring you down.

If God has blessed you, shout it from the housetops! If God brought you up, praise and thank Him! Every time I think about what the Lord has done for me, my soul rejoices.

No one can tell your testimony. No one knows what God has done for you. No one knows how far you've come. No one knows what you've been through. But you know it was only by the grace of God that you survived. Don't allow the devil to steal your testimony.

It may have taken you longer than everybody else, but God has given you the victory. Tell others what God has done in your life. The devil would love for you not to tell your testimony. Why? Because if you tell what God has done for you, someone else might get set free.

CONSIDERATIONS

1. God is a God of second and third and fourth chances. How many chances do you give your spouse, coworkers, children, and parents?

   _____

   _____

2. "When God brings you up, no demon in hell can bring you down." When you choose God over what the devil tempts you with, you will be victorious. What has the devil thrown at you lately that you have resisted?

   _____

   _____

   _____

3. No one else can tell your testimony—what God has done for you. Write your testimony now.

_____

_____

4. Write the names of 10 people who should hear your testimony. Write the date that is two weeks from today and determine to tell those people before that date.

_____

_____

_____

_____

_____

_____

_____

_____

_____

_____

5. What difference will it make in the lives of those 10 people after hearing your testimony? Will they be set free too?

_____

_____

_____

_____

_____

MEDITATION

*Be sober, be vigilant; because **your adversary the
devil** walks about like a roaring lion, seeking whom
he may devour* (1 Peter 5:8).

The devil wants to eat you up and spit you out as a
defeated and pitiful person. But remember, *"greater is He*
[God] *who is in you than he* [devil] *who is in the world"* (see
(1 John 4:4).

DAY 9
HIS MERCY ENDURES

*Oh, give thanks to the Lord, for He is good! For **His mercy endures** forever* (Psalm 118:29).

There is not a person alive today who has not benefited from God's mercy. It was God's mercy that prevailed in the Garden of Eden. When Adam and Eve sinned, the Lord could have scrapped everything and started all over again. God was merciful and allowed Adam and Eve to live with the hope that their seed would redeem back what they had lost.

God's mercy prevailed in the wilderness with Moses and the children of Israel. When the Israelites moaned and groaned, their fate could have ended in immediate and total destruction, but God was merciful.

When Jonah refused to go to Nineveh, God could have killed the unwilling prophet and found another to go in his place. It was God's mercy that allowed the fish to swallow Jonah. God knew what was in Jonah just as He knows what is in you and me.

Sometimes God will allow us to fall because in our time of falling we come to realize that without Him we are nothing. We become convinced that it is only by His mercy that we are able to stand.

"...*His mercy endureth for ever. Let the redeemed of the Lord say so...*" (Ps. 107:1-2 KJV). This verse reminds me of the song, "Your Grace and Mercy" by Frank Williams and the Mississippi Mass Choir, which simply says:

Your grace and mercy has brought me through,
And I'm living this moment because of You.
I want to thank You and praise You, too;
Your grace and mercy has brought me through.

CONSIDERATIONS

1. What does God's mercy mean to you? Write what you believe in two to three sentences.

   _____

   _____

   _____

2. A few examples of God's mercy included Adam and Eve, Moses, and Jonah. List five additional biblical figures who received God's mercy.

   _____

   _____

   _____

   _____

   _____

3. Write two examples of how God's mercy saved you from destruction.

_____

_____

_____

_____

4. Have you received mercy from another who placed conditions on you afterward? Write about this experience and how it differs from God's merciful spirit.

_____

_____

_____

_____

5. "...*His mercy endureth for ever. Let the redeemed of the Lord say so...*" (Ps. 107:1-2 KJV). Write this verse in your own words.

_____

_____

MEDITATION

*Oh, give thanks to the Lord, for He is good! For **His mercy endures** forever* (Psalm 118:29).

God's mercy isn't good for only one day or week or year; His mercy begins at conception and lasts throughout your lifetime and into the next.

DAY 10
STRENGTH TO STAND

*Who are you to judge another's servant? To his
own master he stands or falls. Indeed, he will
be made to stand, for **God is able to make him
stand*** (Romans 14:4).

D
o you believe God is able to pick you up and make
you stand? Until you know that God is able, you
will never cry out for help.

God wants us to understand that there is no lack of
strength in Him. You may not have much of a prayer life, but
God says, "Has thou not known?" In other words, you
should have known that He would take care of you.

The Word says that the everlasting God, Creator of the
universe, is all-powerful. He has brought you through many

problems, so don't let satan deceive you into thinking that it was just luck or coincidence that delivered you.

Remember what God has done for you. If you can't seem to remember anything He has done for you personally, then look around at others who have been delivered out of situations worse than yours. See what God did for them and tell yourself, "If He can do it for them, I know He can do it for me." God's divine love and power brought them through, and He will do the same for you.

God says, "I have the strength that is necessary to escalate and motivate and move you up and out of your circumstances."

If you want to be victorious in all your endeavors, then don't lean on your own understanding or to your own devices or innovations. Instead, in all your ways acknowledge the Lord, and He will direct your path.

CONSIDERATIONS

1. "Do you believe God is able to pick you up and make you stand? Until you know that God is able, you will never cry out for help." Do you believe this statement?

   _____

   _____

   _____

2. God delivers those who believe. Write about a time when others said, "What a coincidence!" or "Wow, what good luck!" but you knew that it was God who made it happen.

   _____

   _____

   _____

3. List five situations that God has brought you through. Thank Him for each deliverance.

_____

_____

_____

_____

_____

4. Leaning only on your own strength will get you along in life, but leaning on the everlasting arms of God will cause you to soar higher and longer in your family relations, career, ministry, community, and all areas of your life. Start leaning on Him today.

_____

5. Write about an area in your life that is frustrating you. Have you been trying to solve it without God's help?

_____

_____

_____

MEDITATION

*Who are you to judge another's servant? To his own master he stands or falls. Indeed, he will be made to stand, for **God is able to make him stand*** (Romans 14:4).

God gives you the strength to stand in the midst of turmoil and walk through it victoriously!

DAY 11
POWER TO THE WEAK

*He gives **power to the weak**, and to those who have
no might He increases strength* (Isaiah 40:29).

The Bible says that God *"gives power to the weak
[faint], and to those who have no might He increases
strength"* (Isa. 40:29). He is saying, "I won't kill you
because you fainted or are weak. I give power to the weak."

When you start losing the strength you once had, you
are fainting. When you can hardly stand up and you begin to
stagger in the throes of sin, lust, envy, and strife, God
declares, "I give power to you!"

If you have looked inside yourself and cannot muster the
strength to get up, God says, "I will increase your strength."

God will not only raise you up, but He'll give you enough power to pull yourself up if you stumble again. He won't help you up so you can be handicapped the rest of your life. No. He gives power to the faint, and to those who are weak He gives strength.

Are you weak with no willpower, no strength, no ability within yourself to resist the enemy? When your body gets tired, remember God and His strength. When satan begins to attack you, remember the power of God residing within your innermost being. Remember that God does not faint or grow weary. In fact, the Holy One does not even sleep.

CONSIDERATIONS

1. "When you can hardly stand up and you begin to stagger in the throes of sin, lust, envy, and strife, God declares, 'I give power to you!'" Have you asked God for His power lately?

   _____

2. God raises you up and gives you enough power to pull yourself up if you stumble again. All Christians stumble their entire lifetime. Thank God that He is faithful to give you power and strength time after time.

3. Do you feel as if you have no willpower, no strength, no ability to resist the enemy? Call out to God with the truth of the situation. He will respond.

   _____

4. The power of God resides within your innermost being. Tap into it constantly to resist the devil's temptations.

5. No matter the time of day or night, God is available. Reach out to Him for help—He never sleeps.

MEDITATION

*He gives **power to the weak**, and to those who have
no might He increases strength* (Isaiah 40:29).

He will increase your strength and give you power
when you acknowledge His lordship in your life and obey
His commandments.

Day 12
All the Doors Were Opened

*But at midnight Paul and Silas were praying and singing hymns to God, and the prisoners were listening to them. Suddenly there was a great earthquake, so that the foundations of the prison were shaken; and immediately **all the doors were opened** and everyone's chains were loosed* (Acts 16:25-26).

As you read this, you may feel that life is passing you by. You often experience success in one area and gross defeat in others. You need a burning desire for the future, the kind of desire that overcomes past fear and inhibitions. You will remain chained to your past and all the secrets therein until you decide: enough is enough! I am telling you that when your desire for the future peaks, you can break out of prison. I challenge you to sit down and write

30 things you would like to do with your life and scratch them off, one by one, as you accomplish them. There is no way you can plan for the future and dwell in the past at the same time. I feel an earthquake coming into your prison! It is midnight—the turning point of days! It is your time for a change. Praise God and escape out of the dungeons of your past.

Don't allow the enemy to plug into you and violate you through his subtle seductions. He is a giver and he is looking for a receiver. You must discern his influence if you are going to rebuke him. Anything that comes, any mood that is not in agreement with God's Word, is satan trying to plug into the earthly realm through your life. He wants you to believe you cannot change. He loves prisons and chains! Statements like, "This is just the way I am" or "I am in a terrible mood today" come from lips that accept what they ought to reject. Never allow yourself to settle for anything less than the attitude God wants you to have in your heart. Don't let satan have your day, your spouse, or your home. Adam and Eve could have put the devil out!

CONSIDERATIONS

1. Do you think that life is passing you by? What fears and inhibitions are keeping you from fulfilling your destiny?

   _____

   _____

2. "Write 30 things you would like to do with your life and scratch them off, one by one, as you accomplish them." Start doing this today.

   _____

   _____

   _____

   _____

   _____

3. "There is no way you can plan for the future and dwell in the past at the same time." What things in your past are keeping you from moving forward in your career, ministry, or family relations?

_____

_____

4. "Anything that comes, any mood that is not in agreement with God's Word, is satan trying to plug into the earthly realm through your life. He wants you to believe you cannot change." Have you believed these lies? Stop today.

_____

5. "This is just the way I am" or "I am in a terrible mood today" are examples of statements that keep you chained. List other examples that you will delete from your language so you can live a free and abundant life.

_____

_____

_____

MEDITATION

*But at midnight Paul and Silas were praying
and singing hymns to God, and the prisoners were
listening to them. Suddenly there was a great earthquake, so that the foundations of the prison were
shaken; and immediately **all the doors were
opened** and everyone's chains were loosed* [broken]
(Acts 16:25-26).

When the chains are tightening around you, remember
that praying and singing hymns to God will break the chains
and open the doors!

DAY 13
BELIEVE IN HIS NAME

But as many as received Him, to them He gave the
*right to become children of God, to those who **believe***
***in His name** (John 1:12).*

I pray that we as Christians never lose our conviction that God does change lives. We must protect this message. Our God enables us to make the radical changes necessary for fulfilling our purposes and responsibilities. Like the caterpillar that eats and sleeps its way into change, the process occurs gradually but nonetheless powerfully. Many people who will rock this world are sleeping in the cocoon of obscurity, waiting for their change to come. The Scriptures declare, *"...it is high time to awake out of sleep: for now is our salvation nearer than when we believed"* (Rom. 13:11 KJV).

A memory of my twin sons playing on the floor when they were children tailors the continuity of this text for me. They were playing with a truck, contributing all the sounds of grinding gears and roaring engines. I didn't pay much attention as I began unwinding from the day's stresses and challenges. Distractedly, I glanced down at the floor and noticed that the boys were now running an airplane down an imaginary runway. I asked, "What happened to the truck you were playing with?"

They explained, "Daddy, this is a transformer!"

I then inquired, "What is a transformer?"

Their answer brought me into the Presence of the Lord. They said, "It can be transformed from what it was before into whatever we want it to be!"

Are you being transformed through believing in His name?

CONSIDERATIONS

1. God enables you to make the radical changes necessary for fulfilling your purposes and responsibilities. What is your God-given destiny? Write it and believe it.

   _____

   _____

   _____

2. "Like the caterpillar that eats and sleeps its way into change, the process occurs gradually but nonetheless powerfully." What gradual changes are taking place in your life?

   _____

   _____

   _____

3. Why should you believe in the name of Jesus? How important is Jesus in your life?

_____

_____

_____

_____

4. "...[I]t is high time to awake out of sleep: for now is our salvation nearer than when we believed" (Rom. 13:11 KJV). Are there areas in your life that you need to awaken?

_____

_____

5. What type of transformation can you feel taking place in your spiritual life?

_____

_____

_____

_____

MEDITATION

*But as many as received Him, to them He gave the
right to become children of God, to those who **believe
in His name*** (John 1:12).

Do you believe in His name enough to become a child
of God?

DAY 14
THE FIRST TRANSFORMER

Before I formed you in the womb I knew you; before you were born I sanctified you; I ordained you a prophet to the nations (Jeremiah 1:5).

I realized that God had made the first transformer. He created man from dust. He created him in such a way that, if need be, He could pull a woman out of him without ever having to reach back into the dust. Out of one creative act God transformed the man into a marriage. Then He transformed the marriage into a family, the family into a society, et cetera.

God never had to reach into the ground again, because the power to transform was intrinsically placed into man. All types of potential were locked into our spirits before birth. For the Christian, transformation at its optimum is the outworking of the internal. God placed certain things in us that must come out. We house the prophetic power of God. Every word of our personal prophetic destiny is inside us. He has ordained us to be.

Only when we are weary from trying to unlock our own resources do we come to the Lord, receive Him, and allow Him to release in us the power to become whatever we need to be. Actually, isn't that what we want to know—our purpose? Then we can use the power to become who we really are. Life has chiseled many of us into mere fragments of who we were meant to be. To all who receive Him, Christ gives the power to slip out of who they were forced into being so they can transform into the individual they each were created to be.

CONSIDERATIONS

1. God transformed a man into a couple into a family into a society. How has He transformed you?

   _____

   _____

   _____

2. Are you being transformed or are you stuck in the same self? What steps can you take to keep moving forward to total transformation?

   _____

   _____

   _____

   _____

3. All types of potential were locked into your spirit before your birth. Are you living up to your potential? Why or why not?

_____

_____

_____

_____

_____

4. Are you weary from trying to unlock your own resources? Go to the Lord, receive Him, and allow Him to release the power within you to become what He created you to be. List five strengths you have from God.

_____

_____

_____

_____

_____

5. Christ gives you the power to slip out of who you were forced into being so you can transform into the individual you were created to be. Take advantage of that power.

MEDITATION

Before I formed you in the womb I knew you; before you were born I sanctified you; I ordained you a prophet to the nations (Jeremiah 1:5).

You serve the First Transformer!

Day 15
Be Transformed

*And do not be conformed to this world, but **be transformed** by the renewing of your mind, that you may prove what is that good and acceptable and perfect will of God* (Romans 12:2).

Many individuals in the Body of Christ are persevering without progressing. They wrestle with areas that have been conformed to the world instead of transformed. This is particularly true of us Pentecostals who often emphasize the gifts of the Spirit and exciting services. It is imperative that, while we keep our mode of expression, we understand that transformation doesn't come from inspiration. Many times preachers sit down after ministering a very inspiring sermon feeling that they accomplished more than they actually did. Transformation takes place in the mind.

The Bible teaches that we are to be renewed by the transforming of our minds (see Eph. 4:23). Only the Holy Spirit knows how to renew the mind. The struggle we have inside us is with our self-perception. Generally our perception of ourselves is affected by those around us. Our early opinion of ourselves is deeply affected by the opinions of the authoritative figures in our formative years. If our parents tended to neglect or ignore us, it tears at our self-worth. Eventually, though, we mature to the degree where we can walk in the light of our own self-image, without it being diluted by the contributions of others.

The Lord wants to help you realize who you are and what you are graced to do. When you understand that He is the only One who really knows you, then you pursue Him with fierceness and determination. Pursue Him!

CONSIDERATIONS

1. Are you keeping track of your transformation? Do you know when you've stopped progressing?

   _____

   _____

   _____

2. Transformation doesn't come from inspiration; transformation takes place in the mind. What does this statement mean to you? Write two to three sentences of explanation.

   _____

   _____

   _____

   _____

3. Only the Holy Spirit knows how to renew your mind. Have you given the Holy Spirit open and welcome access to your mind, body, and spirit? Why or why not?

_____

_____

_____

_____

4. Your opinion of yourself is affected by the opinions of the authoritative figures in your formative years. Have you overcome the adverse affects of parents who may not have been stellar examples of good caregivers?

_____

_____

5. Do you realize that God is the only One who really knows you?

_____

_____

MEDITATION

*And do not be conformed to this world, but **be transformed** by the renewing of your mind, that you may prove what is that good and acceptable and perfect will of God* (Romans 12:2).

Are you conforming more to "this world" than being transformed into becoming the person God created you to be?

DAY 16
CHRIST IS FORMED IN YOU

*My little children, for whom I labor in birth again until **Christ is formed in you** (Galatians 4:19).*

Thank God that He understands the hidden part within each of us. He understands the child in us, and He speaks to our blanket-clutching, thumb-sucking, infantile need. In spite of our growth, income, education, or notoriety, He still speaks to the childhood issues of the aging heart. This is the ministry that only a Father can give.

Have you ever noticed that you are never a grown-up to the ones who birthed you? They completely disregard the gray hairs, crowfeet, and bulging, blossoming waistlines of abundant life. No matter how many children call you "Dad" or "Mom," to your parents you are still just a child yourself.

They seem to think you have slipped into the closet to put on grown-up clothes and are really just playing a game. They must believe that somewhere beneath the receding hairline there is still a child, hiding in the darkness of adulthood. The worst part about it is (keep this quiet) I think they are right!

The Lord looks beyond our facade and sees the trembling places in our lives. He knows our innermost needs. No matter how spiritually mature we try to appear, He is still aware that lurking in the shadows is a discarded candy wrapper from the childish desire we just prayed off last night—the lingering evidence of some little temper or temptation that only the Father can see hiding within His supposedly "all grown-up" little child.

It is He alone whom we must trust to see the very worst in us, yet still think the very best of us. It is simply the love of a Father.

CONSIDERATIONS

1. Do you ever feel like a blanket-clutching, thumb-sucking infant when you face a serious situation? Do you believe that your Father God is willing and able to provide for your every need in whatever state you are in?

   _____

   _____

2. Do your parents still think of you as a child? Or do you still think of your children as children rather than adults with families of their own? Does this thinking hinder or help your relationships?

   _____

   _____

   _____

3. Do you sometimes think that you are only playing "dress-up" as a Christian? Do you compare yourself with other "model" Christians?

_____

_____

_____

_____

_____

4. What or who is lurking in the shadows of your life that keeps Christ from being completely formed in you?

_____

_____

5. God alone sees the very worst in you, yet still thinks the very best of you. Does God see Christ in you?

_____

_____

MEDITATION

*My little children, for whom I labor in birth again until **Christ is formed in you*** (Galatians 4:19).

How much of Christ has been formed in you?

DAY 17
YOU WILL RECEIVE POWER

*But **you shall receive power** when the Holy Spirit
has come upon you; and you shall be witnesses to Me
in Jerusalem, and in all Judea and Samaria, and to
the end of the earth* (Acts 1:8).

Believers must understand the ministry of the Holy
Spirit so they can carry out the will of God for their
lives.

We aren't alone when we lie down at night or go through
the storms of life. When we go through a valley or through a
trial, the Holy Spirit is there to defend us. God will never
leave us nor forsake us (see Heb. 13:5). Jesus is with us to the
end of this age (see Matt. 28:20). When we receive the fullness of the Holy Spirit, we receive an eternal Friend. Jesus is

praying that you have an intimate relationship with the Holy Spirit.

Many friends stay with us until we mess up or until we disagree with them. They quickly leave as if they never knew us. But the Holy Spirit, our Comforter, stays with us forever.

The Holy Spirit does not come and go based upon the circumstances of our lives. He is there when we do well; He is there when we fail. When we are on top of things, He is there. When things are on top of us, He is there. No matter what the situation, the Holy Spirit is always there to help us.

In the same way that Jesus helped the disciples, the Holy Spirit now helps you.

CONSIDERATIONS

1. When you go through a valley or through a trial, the Holy Spirit defends you. Remember a time of trouble when you felt His presence. Write about it.

_____

_____

_____

_____

_____

_____

2. When you receive the fullness of the Holy Spirit, you receive an eternal Friend. Friends in life come and go, but God will never leave you or

forsake you. Remember a friend whom you no longer hear from. Write about the loss.

_____

_____

_____

_____

_____

_____

3. Some friends stay with you until you mess up or until you disagree, then they quickly leave as if they never knew you. How is your relationship with the Holy Spirit different from these types of friends?

_____

_____

_____

4. Write the attributes of a "perfect" friend (for example: loyal, sympathetic, sense of humor,

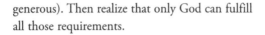

generous). Then realize that only God can fulfill all those requirements.

_____

_____

_____

5. Jesus helped the disciples understand life and God. How does the Holy Spirit help you understand life and God?

_____

_____

_____

MEDITATION

*But **you shall receive power** when the Holy Spirit
has come upon you; and you shall be witnesses to Me
in Jerusalem, and in all Judea and Samaria, and to
the end of the earth* (Acts 1:8).

Open wide your heart, spirit, and mind to receive the
power to strengthen your faith.

Day 18
Riches in Glory

*And my God shall supply all your need according
to His **riches in glory** by Christ Jesus*
(Philippians 4:19).

God says you are worthy to receive the baptism of the
Holy Spirit. Jesus has prayed for you to receive the
Comforter. Is it based upon your merit? Of course
not. You never have and never will live up to the expectations
of a holy God. Jesus, who *"ever liveth to make intercession,"*
prays confidently because He died in your stead (see Heb.
7:25 KJV).

Many have made the baptism of the Holy Spirit and the
Spirit-filled life so difficult when actually it is quite simple.
Many have taught that if you wait long enough, if you pray
hard enough, if you lift your hands, sell out, hold on or hold

out, then you will receive the Holy Spirit. While their intentions may be good, their approach is not scriptural.

We can conclude three things regarding receiving the Holy Spirit:

1. Jesus is praying for you to receive.

2. You must experience a Passover before you can receive.

3. If you have had a Passover, you're a worthy candidate to receive the power of Pentecost.

If you have these three things working for you—the prayers of Jesus, the pleading of the blood in His Passover, and anticipation for the power of Pentecost—you are a worthy candidate.

CONSIDERATIONS

1. Have you received the baptism of the Holy Spirit?

   _____

2. "Jesus has prayed for you to receive the Comforter." What is this gift based on?

   _____

3. What do you think about the following statement? "Many have taught that if you wait long enough, if you pray hard enough, if you lift your hands, sell out, hold on or hold out, that you will receive the Holy Spirit." Write your thoughts.

   _____

   _____

   _____

4. "If you have these three things working for you—the prayers of Jesus, the pleading of the blood in His Passover, and anticipation for the power of Pentecost—you are a worthy candidate." Do you believe you are a worthy candidate? Why or why not?

_____

_____

_____

_____

_____

_____

5. Are you living a riches-in-glory, Spirit-filled life? What do these expressions mean to you?

_____

_____

_____

_____

_____

MEDITATION

*And my God shall supply all your need according to
His **riches in glory** by Christ Jesus*
(Philippians 4:19).

Never doubt His love for you and His desire to supply
all your needs.

DAY 19
ASK, SEEK, KNOCK

*So I say to you, **ask**, and it will be given to you; **seek**, and you will find; **knock**, and it will be opened to you. For everyone who asks receives, and he who seeks finds, and to him who knocks it will be opened* (Luke 11:9-10).

God will not let your needs and wants go unattended, especially when you desire to be more like Him.

Jesus said that those who seek shall find. Seek means to desire. Jesus wants us to desire the Holy Spirit. Would you ask someone for something and have your head or hand turned the other way? Jesus wants our hearts to be lined up with what our lips are saying.

The Holy Spirit, His power, and the change that He alone can bring in your life must be so precious that you will not accept a counterfeit. Nothing else will suffice. Is your heart focused with a desire that will not take "no" for an answer? Do you really want the power of the Holy Spirit?

Those who want the power of the Holy Spirit must take a three-step approach: ask, seek, and knock. What prompts you to open your front door? When someone knocks, you see who it is and what they want.

Jesus said to knock.

Before knocking, you must have a desire to ask. This driving desire caused you to come to the door with great expectation and determination. You searched until you found the door and now you knock.

It may seem that Jesus has these steps out of order, but that's not true. If you have no will to ask, there's no reason to knock. Without the will to seek, there's no reason to knock. Knocking is preceded by a will to ask and search diligently. Knocking gives you access to what you have diligently sought.

CONSIDERATIONS

1. Do you really want the power of the Holy Spirit?
   Have you asked for it?

   _____

   _____

2. How do you think your life will change after you
   receive the baptism of the Holy Spirit? Or, how
   has your life changed after receiving the baptism
   of the Holy Spirit?

   _____

   _____

3. Are you standing at the door knocking with
   expectation and determination?

   _____

4. Are you afraid that the door *will* open? Are you afraid that the door *will not* open?

_____

_____

_____

5. Pray for understanding about your fears. List them here and cross them off after God gives you the answers.

_____

_____

_____

_____

MEDITATION

*So I say to you, **ask**, and it will be given to you; **seek**, and you will find; **knock**, and it will be opened to you. For everyone who asks receives, and he who seeks finds, and to him who knocks it will be opened* (Luke 11:9-10).

Are you asking, seeking, and knocking? If not, start today.

DAY 20
HOW MUCH MORE

An earthly father can be very biased. Sometimes he is stubborn, and sometimes he gives for all the wrong reasons. Jesus made it very clear—if the child asks for one thing, the Father will not give another. He then asked a question:

> *If you then, being evil, know how to give good gifts to your children, **how much more** will your heavenly Father give the Holy Spirit to those who ask Him!* (Luke 11:13)

The emphasis is on "how much more."

God knows that we need the power of the Holy Spirit. Spiritual gifts function only as the Holy Spirit empowers the child of God. As you ask and seek, remember that God knows your motives. He endues you with the power of the Holy Spirit to give you victory over satan, to make you joyful, and to enable you to function in the gifts of the Spirit.

God wants you to have the power of the Holy Spirit. He gives us a simple, three-step approach: ask, seek, and knock. Take the Word as authoritative. Be like the woman who had lost her precious coin. She wanted it so badly that she searched with a candle and swept her house clean.

Old Testament types have their fulfillment in the New Testament. Daniel wrote about a fourth man in the fiery furnace with the three Hebrew children; Moses spoke of the rock that followed the children of Israel; each Israelite household killed a lamb for their Passover. All of these were types of Christ.

The Holy Spirit is likened to wind or breath:

The wind blows where it wishes, and you hear the sound of it, but cannot tell where it comes from and where it goes. So is everyone who is born of the Spirit (John 3:8).

CONSIDERATIONS

1. "God endues you with the power of the Holy Spirit to give you victory over satan, to make you joyful, and to enable you to function in the gifts of the Spirit." Do you believe this statement? Why or why not?

   _____

   _____

   _____

   _____

2. How motivated are you to ask, seek, and knock for the power of the Holy Spirit?

   _____

   _____

3. Describe the Holy Spirit in your own words.

_____

_____

_____

_____

4. Write about why it is important not to grieve the
   Holy Spirit. (See Ephesians 4:29-31.)

_____

_____

_____

5. Write John 3:8 in your own words.

_____

_____

_____

MEDITATION

*If you then, being evil, know how to give good gifts to your children, **how much more** will your heavenly Father give the Holy Spirit to those who ask Him!*
(Luke 11:13)

Think about the best gift you ever received—then realize that God's gift of the Holy Spirit is worth many times more.

DAY 21
DREAMING DREAMS

*And it shall come to pass in the last days, says God, that I will pour out of My Spirit on all flesh; your sons and your daughters shall prophesy, your young men shall see visions, your old men shall **dream dreams**. And on My menservants and on My maidservants I will pour out My Spirit in those days; and they shall prophesy* (Acts 2:17-18).

The sound from Heaven *"filled all the house where they were sitting"* (see Acts 2:2). This sound was a sign, witnessing that Heaven was speaking. The Greek word for *sound* denotes a loud rumbling or roaring voice, much like the rumbling of a tornado that precedes the storm.

This wind filled closets, bedrooms, bathrooms, upstairs, and downstairs. It filled all the components in the house: jars, glasses, significant and insignificant things. This indicates that anyone can be filled with the Holy Spirit.

We have seen saved Baptists, Methodists, Catholics—all walks of Christian professions—filled with the Holy Spirit with the evidence of speaking with other tongues. The only mandatory prerequisite is that you be a believer—a born-again, blood-washed child of God (see Acts 2:38-39; John 14:17).

What about the place where you are sitting? What about your home church? Is it filled with the Holy Spirit? Has your assembly experienced a Pentecost that is filling everything inside? A person becomes a product of his or her environment. You will begin to resemble whatever you are around, whether it is good or bad.

CONSIDERATIONS

1. The wind filled everything in the house, indicating that anyone can be filled with the Holy Spirit. Do you agree? Why or why not?

   _____

   _____

   _____

2. The only mandatory prerequisite for being filled with the Holy Spirit is that you be a believer—a born-again, blood-washed child of God. Do you agree? Why or why not?

   _____

   _____

   _____

3. *"Then Peter said to them, 'Repent, and let every one of you be baptized in the name of Jesus Christ for the remission of sins; and you shall receive the gift of the Holy Spirit. For the promise is to you and to your children, and to all who are afar off, as many as the Lord our God will call'"* (Acts 2:38-39). Write your thoughts about this Scripture passage.

_____

_____

_____

4. *"The Spirit of truth, whom the world cannot receive, because it neither sees Him nor knows Him; but you know Him, for He dwells with you and will be in you"* (John 14:17). Write your thoughts about the Holy Spirit described in this Scripture passage.

_____

_____

_____

5. Has your assembly experienced a Pentecost that is filling everything inside? Why or why not? Explain.

_____

_____

_____

_____

_____

_____

MEDITATION

*And it shall come to pass in the last days, says God, that I will pour out of My Spirit on all flesh; your sons and your daughters shall prophesy, your young men shall see visions, your old men shall **dream dreams**. And on My menservants and on My maidservants I will pour out My Spirit in those days; and they shall prophesy* (Acts 2:17-18).

God is pouring out His Spirit on all peoples—can you feel the wind blowing?

Day 22
Tame the Tongue

*For we all stumble in many things. If anyone does not stumble in word, he is a perfect man, able also to bridle the whole body. Indeed, we put bits in horses' mouths that they may obey us, and we turn their whole body. Look also at ships: although they are so large and are driven by fierce winds, they are turned by a very small rudder wherever the pilot desires. Even so the tongue is a little member and boasts great things. See how great a forest a little fire kindles! And the tongue is a fire, a world of iniquity. The tongue is so set among our members that it defiles the whole body, and sets on fire the course of nature; and it is set on fire by hell. For every kind of beast and bird, of reptile and creature of the sea, is tamed and has been tamed by mankind. But no man can **tame the tongue**. It is an unruly evil, full of deadly poison* (James 3:2-8).

Let's summarize some of these truths:

1. Every beast and animal has been tamed by humankind except the tongue.

2. If we can control the tongue, we can control the whole body.

3. Very large things can be controlled by something very small.

4. The tongue is a fire.

God often employs natural examples to bring about spiritual understanding. Jesus often used natural, physical, tangible analogies in His parables. He talked about a man who sowed seed, a woman who searched for a lost coin, and servants who invested their master's money—all of these describe the Kingdom of God.

In this passage God uses the tongue to teach truth. The tongue is a fire—something out of control, something that is difficult if not impossible to tame. If we can control the tongue, this enables us to control every aspect of our lives.

CONSIDERATIONS

1. *"Indeed, we put bits in horses' mouths that they may obey us, and we turn their whole body."* A small person can control a large horse by pulling the reins attached to the bits in the horse's mouth. Compare this analogy with how what we say with our mouths can either move us in the right or wrong direction.

   _____

   _____

   _____

   _____

2. *"Look also at ships: although they are so large and are driven by fierce winds, they are turned by a very small rudder wherever the pilot desires."* Explain

137

the comparison between your tongue and a ship's rudder.

_____

_____

_____

_____

_____

_____

3. *"The tongue is so set among our members that it defiles the whole body, and sets on fire the course of nature; and it is set on fire by hell."* Write what this Scripture verse means to you.

_____

_____

_____

_____

4. Have you made a conscious effort to think before you speak? Are you aware of how powerful

your words are to others? What do you think about the old adage, "If you can't say something nice, say nothing at all"?

_____

_____

_____

_____

_____

_____

5. If you can control your tongue, you will be able to control every aspect of your life. What things might be affected in your life?

_____

_____

_____

_____

MEDITATION

*For we all stumble in many things. If anyone does not stumble in word, he is a perfect man, able also to bridle the whole body. Indeed, we put bits in horses' mouths that they may obey us, and we turn their whole body. Look also at ships: although they are so large and are driven by fierce winds, they are turned by a very small rudder wherever the pilot desires. Even so the tongue is a little member and boasts great things. See how great a forest a little fire kindles! And the tongue is a fire, a world of iniquity. The tongue is so set among our members that it defiles the whole body, and sets on fire the course of nature; and it is set on fire by hell. For every kind of beast and bird, of reptile and creature of the sea, is tamed and has been tamed by mankind. But no man can **tame the tongue**. It is an unruly evil, full of deadly poison* (James 3:2-8).

Indeed, we all stumble in word, yet we must tame our tongue if we are to succeed and live victoriously.

DAY 23
AND THEY WILL RECOVER

And these signs will follow those who believe: In My name they will cast out demons; they will speak with new tongues; they will take up serpents; and if they drink anything deadly, it will by no means hurt them; they will lay hands on the sick, **and they will recover** *(Mark 16:17-18).*

Being filled with the Holy Spirit gives us tremendous power for living the Christian life.

The Holy Spirit has not been given to the Church to entertain congregations but rather to empower them. Jesus said, *"Ye shall receive power, after that the Holy Ghost is come upon you…"* (Acts 1:8 KJV). The Holy Spirit gives us power not to just shout, run the aisles, or to put on a show. He empowers us to intervene in society as a witness.

The Book of Acts records the amazing signs and wonders that occurred through the disciples. What was the catalyst for these miracles? Pentecost. After being endued with power from on high, *"They went forth, and preached every where, the Lord working with them, and confirming the word with signs following"* (Mark 16:20 KJV).

That's the kind of power we need to transform our lives, families, churches, and society.

CONSIDERATIONS

1. "The Holy Spirit has not been given to the Church to entertain congregations but rather to empower them." Do you attend a church that has been empowered by the Holy Spirit?

   _____

2. *"Jesus said, 'Ye shall receive power, after that the Holy Ghost is come upon you'"* (Acts 1:8 KJV). The Holy Spirit gives you power not to just shout, run the aisles, or to put on a show. He empowers you as a witness in society. How have you used your power to change your family, community, workplace, state, and country?

   _____

   _____

3. Read the Book of Acts and write about several of the signs and wonders that happened.

_____

_____

_____

4. What signs and wonders caught your attention the most? Why? Write in more depth about how it affected you.

_____

_____

_____

_____

5. *"They went forth, and preached every where, the Lord working with them, and confirming the word with signs following"* (Mark 16:20 KJV). Have you witnessed *"signs following"*? Describe an instance.

_____

_____

MEDITATION

*And these signs will follow those who believe: In My name they will cast out demons; they will speak with new tongues; they will take up serpents; and if they drink anything deadly, it will by no means hurt them; they will lay hands on the sick, **and they will recover*** (Mark 16:17-18).

Do you believe that this Scripture verse is true today or only for times past?

Day 24
Bypass Satan's Radar

*Then I heard a loud voice saying in Heaven, "Now salvation, and **strength**, and the Kingdom of our God, and the power of His Christ have come, for the accuser of our brethren, who accused them before our God day and night, has been cast down"*
(Revelation 12:10).

A CB radio gives you the ability to speak to other people providing you are on the same frequency. Different people use different channels for a variety of reasons. Whatever channel you use to transmit or receive a message, the transmitter and the one receiving must be on the same channel and have the squelch turned up loud enough to hear. CB radios also have a special channel for emergencies. Any time you need the police or emergency assistance you can switch to this frequency and no one else can monitor your conversation.

This may seem like a crude analogy, but in the spirit world many messages are being transmitted. The Bible says that satan is the *"prince of the power of the air"* (see Eph. 2:2). If we stay on the same frequency, he can pick up our transmissions. But satan cannot monitor the emergency channel. His squelch cannot tune in because it is just a bunch of static to him. He cannot make out what we are saying. Praying in the Spirit is a frequency that satan cannot pick up.

Since satan is the prince of the power of the air and comes before the presence of God, he constantly surveys our prayer life. No wonder we experience such adversity and opposition when we try to get close to God. To make our way to the throne of God, we must push past the enemy's surveillance.

CONSIDERATIONS

1. In the spirit world many messages are being transmitted. Because satan is the *"prince of the power of the air"* he can pick up our prayers to God. Have you ever thought that satan is eavesdropping on your conversations with your heavenly Father?

   _____

   _____

2. Praying in the Spirit is a frequency that satan cannot pick up. Does this change your mind about praying in tongues? Or does it confirm what you already knew?

   _____

   _____

151

3. John wrote in Revelation: *"Now salvation, and strength, and the Kingdom of our God, and the power of His Christ have come."* Does this verse give you a sense of comfort and hope? You can have strength for every moment through His Word.

_____

_____

4. One of satan's tactics to keep you from getting closer to God is to keep you from using a frequency he can't hear. What's keeping you from switching channels?

_____

_____

5. To make your way to the throne of God, push past the enemy's surveillance by taking these steps:

_____

_____

MEDITATION

*Then I heard a loud voice saying in Heaven, "Now salvation, and **strength**, and the Kingdom of our God, and the power of His Christ have come, for the accuser of our brethren, who accused them before our God day and night, has been cast down"* (Revelation 12:10).

Remember, the accuser has been cast down!

DAY 25
PROFOUND TRUTHS

In the following passage, we find some of the simplest and most profound truths in all the Word of God. But everything hinges on the truth stated in Jude 20:

> *But you, beloved, **building yourselves up** on your*
> *most holy faith, praying in the Holy Spirit, keep*
> *yourselves in the love of God, looking for the mercy of*
> *our Lord Jesus Christ unto eternal life. And on some*
> *have compassion, making a distinction; but others*
> *save with fear, pulling them out of the fire, hating*
> *even the garment defiled by the flesh (Jude 20-23).*

We can build up ourselves, cultivate a sense of expectancy about the coming of the Lord, have compassion on those who have fallen, and be moved with zeal to make a difference in the lives of those who have spotted their garments.

Let's look at the ability to "build up." The word *build* is an architectural word that means "to cause a building to stand." It means "to lay a good foundation." In the natural realm, it is always important to leave yourself the ability to add on to your building in case you need to expand in the future. If you have outgrown your spiritual house, the Holy Spirit gives you the resources to add on to meet your demands.

If you have a ministry then you have a place to house it, to build on. Are there weak areas in the structure? Build them up. You do this by praying in the Holy Spirit. This will build up your faith so that you can stand against Goliath and know that your God is bigger than the giant who defies you.

CONSIDERATIONS

1. Have you laid a good spiritual foundation in your life? When storms come along, can you stand solidly on the Word of God and His promises?

   _____

   _____

   _____

   _____

2. Have you built a good spiritual structure around your life? When storms come along, can you rest peacefully on the Rock of your salvation?

   _____

   _____

   _____

3. Have you allowed room for expansion of your spiritual life? When storms come along, can you invite others into your safe and loving environment?

_____

_____

_____

4. Have you noticed that while you are building up your spiritual life, your faith has been increasing? Write an example or two of how your faith in Christ has increased over the months or years.

_____

_____

_____

5. Knowing your faith is built on a Rock-solid foundation gives you the power and strength to overcome all obstacles that come your way. Do you believe this?

_____

_____

MEDITATION

*But you, beloved, **building yourselves up** on your
most holy faith, praying in the Holy Spirit, keep
yourselves in the love of God, looking for the mercy of
our Lord Jesus Christ unto eternal life. And on some
have compassion, making a distinction; but others
save with fear, pulling them out of the fire, hating
even the garment defiled by the flesh (Jude 20-23).*

You will receive strength as you build yourself up in
faith, pray in the Holy Spirit, love God and His mercy, have
compassion, and hate sin.

DAY 26
BUILDING UP

For he who speaks in a tongue does not speak to men
but to God, for no one understands him; however, in
the spirit he speaks mysteries. But he who prophesies
speaks edification and exhortation and comfort to
men. He who speaks in a tongue edifies himself, but
*he who prophesies **edifies** the church*
(1 Corinthians 14:2-4).

Your complexes will vanish as the Holy Spirit imparts confidence. Your fears will vanish as the Holy Spirit builds you up. Your past failures and sins will be dealt a decisive blow by the Holy Spirit. This change will take every weak area in your structure and begin to brace and strengthen it, giving you glorious victory.

You may not even notice the change taking place, and you might not even realize it's the Holy Spirit doing the work quietly and internally. But it won't be long before what is happening on the inside begins to manifest itself on the outside.

As you come into a deeper relationship with God, you will find that you cannot survive on a "Now I lay me down to sleep" prayer. Your prayer life will have to match your ministry and commitment to Spirit-filled living.

The best defense against disease is our natural immune system, which has been designed by God to help us ward off the enemies of our body and diseases that come against us. But the immune system must be kept strong and vibrant by eating right, getting plenty of rest, and exercising.

Many of us are at our own lowest ebb spiritually and have become susceptible to anything that comes our way. But if we pray in the Holy Spirit we will be built up, enabling us to fight off sin and discouragement.

CONSIDERATIONS

1. "Your complexes will vanish as the Holy Spirit imparts confidence. Your fears will vanish as the Holy Spirit builds you up." What complexes do you have that you will be glad to see vanish?

   _____

   _____

   _____

2. As the Holy Spirit helps build you up, every weak area in your structure will be braced and strengthened, giving you victory. Can you identify any weak areas where work needs to begin?

   _____

   _____

   _____

3. Does your prayer life match your ministry and commitment to Spirit-filled living? Why or why not?

_____

_____

_____

_____

4. The best defense against disease is your natural immune system. Are you keeping your spiritual immune system strong and vibrant by eating right, getting plenty of rest, and exercising?

_____

_____

_____

_____

5. If you pray in the Holy Spirit, you will be built up and able to fight off sin and discouragement.

MEDITATION

*For he who speaks in a tongue does not speak to men but to God, for no one understands him; however, in the spirit he speaks mysteries. But he who prophesies speaks edification and exhortation and comfort to men. He who speaks in a tongue edifies himself, but he who prophesies **edifies** the church*
(1 Corinthians 14:2-4).

Are you edifying and exhorting yourself or God and the Church?

DAY 27
LIKE A FLOOD

So shall they fear the name of the Lord from the west,
and His glory from the rising of the sun; when the
*enemy comes in **like a flood**, the Spirit of the Lord*
will lift up a standard against him (Isaiah 59:19).

Yes, there are times when the enemy invades our lives. He will come into your mind; he will come into your marriage; he will come into your ministry. He comes in like a flood and desires to devour you and anything that has been born of God in your life.

The Holy Spirit stands by as your ally. When the enemy comes in like a flood, the Spirit lifts up a standard against him. He provides you with a place of defense, a place of shelter, a place of refuge, a place to hide.

Job's life is a good example of this. When God praised Job's integrity, satan pointed out:

Hast not thou made a hedge about him, and about his house, and about all that he hath on every side? (Job 1:10 KJV)

The adversary asked permission to touch all that Job had. Satan came in like a flood, destroying his sons, daughters, servants, and livestock. Not satisfied with this, satan asked permission to afflict Job's body. God set a limit, however, and said, "...save his life" (Job 2:6 KJV).

Praying in the Spirit sets up a wall of defense that satan cannot penetrate. The Spirit will lift up the wall of the blood of Jesus and say, "Satan, you can't touch this!"

CONSIDERATIONS

1. As a child, did you have a special hiding place where your brother, sister, friend, or mom could not find you? God provides you with a place of defense, a place of shelter, a place of refuge, a place to hide. Run to that place when the enemy is tempting you.

   _____

   _____

   _____

   _____

2. *"Hast not thou made a hedge about him, and about his house, and about all that he hath on every side?"* (Job 1:10 KJV). God built a hedge of protection around Job. Imagine a hedge around you, your family, and your home. Feel safe from harm.

3. Why do you think God allowed satan to take Job's family and possessions away from him?

_____

_____

_____

_____

_____

4. Do you ever feel like a flood is washing over you? Do your emotions run wild? Does anger get the best of you? Run to your hiding place behind the hedge of protection.

_____

_____

_____

_____

_____

_____

_____

5. Hiding is not a sign of weakness—it is a step
toward trusting God more and having faith that
He will protect you from your enemy. What are
a few situations that make you run and hide?

_____

_____

_____

_____

_____

MEDITATION

*So shall they fear the name of the Lord from the west, and His glory from the rising of the sun; when the enemy comes in **like a flood**, the Spirit of the Lord will lift up a standard against him* (Isaiah 59:19).

Believe that when the enemy wants to wash over you like a flood, the Spirit of the Lord will hide you in the shelter of His love and keep the waters from overwhelming you.

DAY 28
PRAY AND SING!

*What is the conclusion then? I will **pray** with the spirit, and I will also **pray** with the understanding. I will **sing** with the spirit, and I will also **sing** with the understanding* (1 Corinthians 14:15).

Sometimes we have no knowledge of how to pray because the things that we confront are bigger than we are. They are deeper than our human logic can comprehend.

That's why we need to pray within the spirit realm, which is bigger than any problem, weakness, or dilemma we face. We also need to ask God to interpret to us the things that we have spoken through the auspice of the Holy Spirit. As He reveals them to us, we will gain an understanding.

Sometimes we don't know what to say. Our heart is crushed; our spirit is overwhelmed. We know that we need a touch; we know the area that needs to be touched, but we don't always know what to say.

Have you ever been so overwhelmed, so overcome that all you can do is groan? Maybe you can only say, "Jesus, help me," or "I need You, Lord." That's when we need to change our language. We need to wait on the Holy Spirit because He knows how to pray...and what to pray. The Holy Spirit will always pray in alignment with the will of God (see Rom. 8:27).

The anointing of the Holy Spirit doesn't always bring chills or goose bumps. It isn't always charged with emotion. The anointing, however, brings power and strength.

CONSIDERATIONS

1. Praying within the spirit realm is bigger than any problem, weakness, or dilemma we face. List the biggest problem or weakness you are facing. Now pray or sing it over to God.

_____

_____

_____

2. Sometimes we don't know what to pray to God. Our hearts are crushed and our spirits are overwhelmed. Praying through the Holy Spirit releases our inhibitions. Remember a time when you didn't know how or what to pray. Have you ever sung a prayer to God?

_____

3. When God interprets and reveals to us the things that we have spoken through the auspice of the Holy Spirit, we gain understanding. What does this mean to you?

_____

_____

4. The Holy Spirit always prays in alignment with the will of God. *"Now He who searches the hearts knows what the mind of the Spirit is, because He makes intercession for the saints according to the will of God"* (Romans 8:27). Write this verse in your own words.

_____

_____

5. The anointing of the Holy Spirit brings power and strength. Have you felt this anointing? If not, are you open to experiencing it? Why or why not?

_____

_____

MEDITATION

*What is the conclusion then? I will **pray** with the spirit, and I will also **pray** with the understanding. I will **sing** with the spirit, and I will also **sing** with the understanding* (1 Corinthians 14:15).

Pray and sing with understanding revealed by God through the Holy Spirit.

DAY 29
STRENGTH THROUGH FAITH

But without faith it is impossible to please Him,
for he who comes to God must believe that He is, and
that He is a rewarder of those who diligently seek
Him (Hebrews 11:6).

"I will pray with the understanding" means that as we pray by the unction and leadership of the Holy Spirit, we pray a prayer that will have meaning as the same Holy Spirit interprets to us the things that we have spoken.

The Old Testament high priest knew there was only one place where he could see and experience a manifestation of God's glory and that was in the holy of holies. That's where God promised to show Himself and commune with His people (see Exod. 25:17-22).

In these last days, satan and all his cohorts are waging a final onslaught against the Church. We must know God in a way in which we have never known Him before. Within some of you are miracles, unborn babies, ministries, and gifts. Many of you have callings on your life.

Because of circumstances—perhaps something beyond your control; perhaps because of your faults, failures, or your past life—satan has told you that your baby, your gift, or your ministry must be aborted. But satan is a liar. Scripture tells us *"the gifts and callings of God are without repentance"* (Rom. 11:29 KJV).

You need to get to where you can see the raw, undiluted presence of God and His anointing.

CONSIDERATIONS

1. The manifestation of God's glory was in the holy of holies, where God promised to show Himself and commune with His people (see Exod. 25:17-22). In the New Testament and today, we have direct access to Him through Jesus Christ. Read Exodus 25:17-22 and write what you think about this place God described.

   _____

   _____

2. Do you believe that knowing the God of the Old Testament is as important as knowing the God of the New Testament? Are they the same or a different God? Explain your answer.

   _____

   _____

3. List some things that satan has done to wage war against you.

_____

_____

_____

_____

4. List the ways you foiled satan's attack on you, your gifts, your talents, your family, et cetera.

_____

_____

_____

_____

5. Seek God where you can see the raw, undiluted presence of Him and His anointing.

MEDITATION

But without faith it is impossible to please Him,
for he who comes to God must believe that He is, and
that He is a rewarder of those who diligently seek
Him (Hebrews 11:6).

Pleasing God means having faith in His salvation plan,
obeying Him, and seeking His direction for your life.

DAY 30
RUN WITH ENDURANCE

What encourages me when I go through the storms of life? I look in the Word of God and find that someone else has already been there and made it through. We are surrounded by witnesses:

> *Therefore we also, since we are surrounded by so great a cloud of witnesses, let us lay aside every weight, and the sin which so easily ensnares us, and let us **run with endurance** the race that is set before us*
> (Hebrews 12:1).

Saints have had to get to a certain place before they saw the manifestation of God.

Noah endured a torrential downpour that flooded the earth for months, but he had a place that gave him access to God. On the third level of the ark a window gave him access to the heavenlies.

Jacob struggled for years with who he was compared to who he wanted to be. His wrestling climaxed when he got to Jabbok, which means "to pour out, to empty." Jacob went alone to Jabbok, the place of struggle where he wrestled with an angel. Divinity met with humanity, and Jacob's thigh was put out of joint. Upon arriving at the place, the patriarch was Jacob ("swindler, supplanter, cheater"), but after the struggle, his name was Israel ("prince of God"). It was a place of power, as God gave him power with Himself and humankind (see Gen. 32:21-29).

Like Jacob, you may be struggling with who you are. Some of you may be wrestling with your past. You need to know that there is a place with God of yoke-breaking anointing.

CONSIDERATIONS

1. The Word of God is full of witnesses who have already faced life's storms but continued to run the race successfully. Write about three people whose stories in the Bible are encouraging to you.

   _____

   _____

   _____

2. Saints have had to get to a certain place before they saw the manifestation of God. Noah and Jacob were used as examples. Can you think of other biblical people who saw the manifestation of God?

   _____

   _____

3. Have you witnessed a manifestation of God? Describe it.

_____

_____

_____

4. Imagine meeting God face to face. Write what you think that experience would be like.

_____

_____

_____

_____

_____

5. Most days are you running *toward* God or *away* from God? Why?

_____

_____

_____

_____

MEDITATION

*Therefore we also, since we are surrounded by so great a cloud of witnesses, let us lay aside every weight, and the sin which so easily ensnares us, and let us **run with endurance** the race that is set before us* (Hebrews 12:1).

You may have a "cloud of witnesses" in your family, church, or community who have faced storms, but they continued to run the race. Are you running with endurance?

Day 31
No More Burdens

*It shall come to pass in that day that **his burden will be taken away** from your shoulder, and his yoke from your neck, and the yoke will be destroyed because of the anointing oil* (Isaiah 10:27).

Timely truths from this passage:

1. The anointing flows from the head down (see Ps. 133:2). Jesus is the head. His anointing is flowing, but we must be in alignment (in fellowship) with Him.

2. The anointing will be *"...like the dew of Hermon..."* (Ps. 133:3). The Israelites knew the

191

dew of Mt. Hermon and Mt. Zion was heavy even in dry weather.

3. The anointing will take authority over your situations: *"...For there the Lord commanded the blessing..."* (Ps.133:3).

4. The anointing will lift burdens from your shoulder (see Isa. 10:27).

5. The anointing will take away yokes that have caused you to say and do things and go places you really didn't desire (see Isa. 10:27).

6. The anointing will destroy the yoke. It isn't enough to just lift the yoke from your neck. If you leave a yoke enabled, it can resume its previous position at any time. The anointing dismantles everything that satan had planned for your life.

Everything satan planned to do (his head) and all the things he wanted to do (his hands) has been destroyed by the anointing. He has been cut off and rendered helpless.

CONSIDERATIONS

1. The anointing flows from Jesus, but you must be in fellowship with Him to receive it. What does the anointing mean to you?

   _____

2. The anointing takes authority over your situations. Are you daily giving Jesus authority over your life?

   _____

3. The anointing will take away yokes that have caused you to say and do things and go places you knew were wrong. List some yokes that you want destroyed.

   _____

   _____

4. Everything satan planned to do and all the things he wanted to do to you have been destroyed by the anointing. You have more authority than satan. Are you using it to avoid his snares?

_____

_____

_____

_____

_____

5. Are you physically and spiritually tired? Shake off your heavy yokes unto the God who said, *"Take My yoke upon you and learn from Me, for I am gentle and lowly in heart, and you will find rest for your souls. For My yoke is easy and My burden is light"* (Matt. 11:29-30).

_____

_____

_____

MEDITATION

*It shall come to pass in that day that **his burden will be taken away** from your shoulder, and his yoke from your neck, and the yoke will be destroyed because of the anointing oil* (Isaiah 10:27).

When you are tired inside and out, allow the refreshing oil of anointing to flow over you.

DAY 32
MIRACLES

How shall we escape if we neglect so great a salvation,
which at the first began to be spoken by the Lord,
and was confirmed to us by those who heard Him,
God also bearing witness both with signs and won-
*ders, with various **miracles**, and gifts of the Holy*
Spirit, according to His own will? (Hebrews 2:3-4)

Many try to limit God, saying He has spoken in the past but has ceased to speak today. This, however, is not true. God continues to speak to us through His written Word.

The Holy Spirit also speaks to us today. Tongues are God's message for the last days. It isn't the only way that He can speak, but it is one avenue of speech. We need faith to allow Him to speak and interpret the message through a willing vessel.

We need to get hold of God like never before because He is speaking a vital message in these last days. He is looking for someone to deliver a timely, life-changing Word. Many times, however, it is in secret code and can only be understood by those who have the Holy Spirit.

All the miracles of Christ declared what His followers would do in that day. Because the world did not receive Him, did not see Him, and did not know Him, they crucified the Lord of glory.

Only John went to the cross like Jesus. Is it any wonder that he received an amazing vision known as "The Revelation of Jesus Christ"? Before receiving this vision, he was exiled to the isle of Patmos.

CONSIDERATIONS

1. "The Holy Spirit also speaks to us today. Tongues are God's message for the last days. It isn't the only way that He can speak, but it is one avenue of speech." Do you agree with this statement? Why or why not?

   _____

   _____

2. God is looking for someone to deliver a timely, life-changing Word. Are you that someone?

   _____

   _____

3. Many times His timely, life-changing Word is in secret code and can only be understood by those

who have the Holy Spirit. Do you agree with this statement? Why or why not?

_____

_____

_____

_____

_____

4. Do you need to see signs and wonders and various miracles to believe God is real?

_____

_____

5. Are the gifts of the Holy Spirit only for a chosen few or all believers? Explain your answer.

_____

_____

_____

_____

_____

MEDITATION

*How shall we escape if we neglect so great a salvation,
which at the first began to be spoken by the Lord,
and was confirmed to us by those who heard Him,
God also bearing witness both with signs and wonders, with various **miracles**, and gifts of the Holy
Spirit, according to His own will?* (Hebrews 2:3-4)

God is speaking a vital message in these last days. Are
you listening?

Day 33
Strength for Every Moment

*If you love Me, keep My commandments. And I will pray the Father, and He will give you another Helper, that He may abide with you forever—the Spirit of truth, whom the world cannot receive, because it neither sees Him nor knows Him; but you know Him, for He dwells with you and will be in you. **I will not leave you** orphans; I will come to you* (John 14:15-18).

This Scripture indicates the Kingdom of God was going through some drastic changes.

1. We find the changing of the guard. *"I will pray the Father, and He shall give you another Comforter"* (John 14:16 KJV). *Another* in this passage means another one just like Jesus. He confirmed

this in the very next verse: *"Ye know Him [the Spirit of truth]; for He dwelleth with you, and shall be in you"* (John 14:17 KJV).

2. We find an obligation on our part to receive the Holy Spirit. Jesus said, *"If ye love Me, keep My commandments"* (John 14:15 KJV). As a result of our walking in obedience, Jesus said that He would pray to the Father. He in turn would send another Comforter to us.

3. Jesus said three things about the Holy Spirit in John 14:17:

- The world cannot receive Him.

- The world cannot see Him, because His ways are not their ways; He is a mystery to them.

- The world doesn't know Him.

Why aren't more believers hearing from God? Many are not walking in obedience and do not have the fullness of the Holy Spirit. Jesus only reveals His secrets to those who are trustworthy and have intimate fellowship with Him.

CONSIDERATIONS

1. Jesus comforted His disciples, and the Holy Spirit has been sent to comfort you. Have you felt His presence in the heat of the fire and the throes of the storm?

   _____

   _____

2. There is an obligation on your part to receive the Holy Spirit. Jesus said, *"If ye love Me, keep My commandments."* Have you asked to receive the Holy Spirit? Why or why not?

   _____

   _____

   _____

3. Why do you think the world cannot receive the Holy Spirit?

_____

_____

_____

4. Why is the Holy Spirit a mystery to the world of unbelievers?

_____

_____

_____

5. Why doesn't the world know the Holy Spirit? Do you know the Holy Spirit?

_____

_____

_____

_____

_____

MEDITATION

*If you love Me, keep My commandments. And I will
pray the Father, and He will give you another Helper,
that He may abide with you forever—the Spirit of
truth, whom the world cannot receive, because it neither sees Him nor knows Him; but you know Him,
for He dwells with you and will be in you. **I will not
leave you** orphans; I will come to you*
(John 14:15-18).

Jesus only reveals His secrets to those who are trustworthy and have intimate fellowship with Him. Is He revealing
His secrets to you?

DAY 34
YOU WILL KNOW

*At that day **you will know** that I am in My Father,
and you in Me, and I in you* (John 14:20).

J esus told His disciples that the world would not understand, see, or know, but those who had the Holy Spirit
would.

What He was saying can be paraphrased: "At that day
they will see me as dead, but you will know that I am still in
control. When they bury Me in a tomb, some will say it's
over. But you will know I spoke mysteries the world could
not understand. *'Destroy this temple and in three days I will
raise it up.'* When they come on that first Easter morning
and find My body gone, they will say it was stolen. You will
know that I have risen from the dead. My ministry will continue through the Holy Spirit."

"At that day you will know" denotes something progressive. *"Then shall we know, if we follow on to know the Lord..."* (Hos. 6:3 KJV). *"Ye shall know the truth..."* (John 8:32 KJV). *"...When I became a man..."* denotes something that isn't complete but is in the making (see 1 Cor. 13:11 KJV).

Apostle Paul wrote about Kingdom revelation that staggers the mind. The truth is spoken and revealed in secret code. We must understand the code. But as it is written:

> *...Eye hath not seen, nor ear heard, neither have entered into the heart of man, the things which God hath prepared for them that love Him. But God hath revealed them unto us by His Spirit: for the Spirit searcheth all things, yea, the deep things of God* (1 Corinthians 2:9-10 KJV).

CONSIDERATIONS

1. "Jesus told His disciples that the world would not understand, see, or know, but those who had the Holy Spirit would." Have there been times when you understood and situation more clearly than anyone else involved? God may have been revealing things to only you. Describe your experience. Or, watch carefully for this to happen to you and remember His goodness.

   _____

   _____

   _____

   _____

2. Life is full of indecisions, but *you will know* that the Lord is your Shepherd when you sincerely

seek His face. Have you sought Him in earnest lately? Do so today.

_____

_____

3. Many claim to know "the truth" when all they really know is what the world preaches. Knowing the Truth is knowing God through His Word and the Holy Spirit. Do you know the Truth that will set you free?

_____

_____

_____

4. *"Eye hath not seen, nor ear heard, neither have entered into the heart of man, the things which God hath prepared for them that love Him."* How can you prepare your heart and mind to receive the mysteries of God?

_____

_____

_____

5. *"But God hath revealed them unto us by His Spirit: for the Spirit searcheth all things, yea, the deep things of God."* How deeply do you want to know the deep things of God?

_____

_____

MEDITATION

*At that day **you will know** that I am in My Father,
and you in Me, and I in you* (John 14:20).

When you know that you know that you know Jesus is
Lord, He will be in you and you in Him.

Day 35
The Light of Life

*Then Jesus spoke to them again, saying, "I am the light of the world. He who follows Me shall not walk in darkness, but have **the light of life**"* (John 8:12).

As the Church allows the Holy Spirit to work in and through us, the world will begin to see Jesus and the Kingdom of God in action. It will be a mystery to the world but a powerful reality to the Church. But it won't happen overnight. It's progressive, day by day, trial by trial, storm by storm, valley by valley, and temptation by temptation.

When He died, darkness covered the earth. Except for the Holy Spirit, darkness would prevail. But as the Body of Christ allows the Holy Spirit to fill every fiber of our being, we become the light of the world.

We are beacons, a lighthouse to a world of storm-tossed, beaten, battered individuals. We are to be a city set on a hill and illuminated by the Holy Spirit. Our joy, our peace, and our righteousness should shine brightly, encouraging others to find a refuge in our God. The fruit of the Spirit in our lives will act as a magnet and draw them to Jesus.

When Jesus walked the earth, He was a preservative for this world. A thief could not die without first being preserved by His forgiveness; a widow's only son, the apple of her eye, could not reach the gates of death without Jesus stopping the funeral procession; Lazarus could not lay decomposing in a tomb without hearing a voice, *"Lazarus, come forth!"* (John 11:43).

CONSIDERATIONS

1. As the Holy Spirit works in and through you, the world will begin to see Jesus and the Kingdom of God in action. Write about a time or two when you did something that the world did not understand, but Jesus was honored and glorified.

_____

_____

_____

_____

_____

2. "When Jesus died, darkness covered the earth. Except for the Holy Spirit, darkness would prevail." But because of the Holy Spirit in His

believers, light prevails. Where have you shone His light lately?

_____

_____

3. Do you see yourself as a beacon, a lighthouse to a world of storm-tossed, beaten, battered individuals? Are you a city set on a hill and illuminated by the Holy Spirit? Why or why not?

_____

_____

_____

_____

4. Your joy, peace, and righteousness should shine brightly, encouraging others to find a refuge in your God. Is this so?

_____

_____

_____

5. Write what you think it was like for Lazarus who lay dead in a tomb to hear the voice of Jesus as He called his name.

_____

_____

_____

_____

_____

_____

MEDITATION

*Then Jesus spoke to them again, saying, "I am the light of the world. He who follows Me shall not walk in darkness, but have **the light of life**" (John 8:12).*

Walk out of the darkness and into the Light of Life today.

Day 36
God of Peace

*For **God** is not the author of confusion but **of peace**,
as in all the churches of the saints*
(1 Corinthians 14:33).

The Corinthian church didn't have a problem with spirituality but with order. There must be a balance. We need Spirit-filled churches, but we also need Word-filled churches that have the wisdom to know how to function.

Is it any wonder that satan battles the gifts and manifestations of the Holy Spirit? He knows the gifts of the Spirit are going to cause the Church to perform signs, bringing the Gospel to our troubled, chaotic society.

God is looking for a Church that believes He can confirm them and their ministry with gifts, signs, and wonders in the Holy Spirit. (See Hebrews 2:3-4 and Mark 16:17-18.)

Don't be dismayed if those who see you say, "These people are fanatics!" The Holy Spirit will cause a division between truth and falsehood. When you begin to function in the gift of God for your life and the devil sees a true manifestation of the Holy Spirit, expect to be put on the devil's hit list. This is nothing more than a trick of the enemy to get you to stop.

Many church folks have followed the path of society. We live in a fast-food world where nobody wants to wait. Even church people want a quick fix. We want power without pursuing the Power Giver. But anyone who has ever been mightily anointed of God has had to pursue God.

CONSIDERATIONS

1. "We need Spirit-filled churches, but we also need Word-filled churches that have the wisdom to know how to function." Do you attend or have you attended a church where confusion reigned? Why do you think that happens?

   _____

   _____

   _____

   _____

2. Satan battles the gifts and manifestations of the Holy Spirit because he knows the gifts of the Spirit bring the Gospel to our troubled, chaotic society. Have you noticed satan attacking people

who are using their gifts? Have you noticed that God is victorious over all of satan's attacks?

_____

_____

_____

3. "The Holy Spirit will cause a division between truth and falsehood." What do you do when people say things against what you feel the Lord is telling you to be the truth?

_____

_____

_____

4. "We live in a fast-food world where nobody wants to wait." List a few examples of life in your "fast-food world."

_____

_____

_____

5. Receiving power and strength from God takes time to pursue Him. Will you slow down enough today to enjoy the God of peace?

_____

_____

MEDITATION

*For **God** is not the author of confusion but **of peace**,*
as in all the churches of the saints
(1 Corinthians 14:33).

God will not cause you to feel confused or worried. He is the God of peace. Seek Him out for a time of refreshment together.

DAY 37
CONSUMING FIRE

So Elijah answered and said to the captain of fifty,
"If I am a man of God, then let fire come down from
Heaven and consume you and your fifty men." And
***fire came down from Heaven and consumed** him*
and his fifty (2 Kings 1:10).

The fire of God consumed this messenger and his fifty men, then another captain with his fifty.

We need to have the same spirit as Elijah. When tempted to align ourselves with the world, we must tell the devil, "I cannot and will not come down!" All too often people are so close to the devil that they are not intimidating his kingdom at all. But when the Kingdom of Light stands in unity, the kingdom of darkness comes down.

God is definitely speaking to His people. The question is: Can we hear Him? The Holy Spirit is speaking right now. He is speaking words of truth and guidance. He speaks what He hears in Heaven.

Whenever the Holy Spirit speaks, He testifies that He has been in the boardroom of Heaven. Hearing from Him causes us to lift our head. Just when satan thought he had you, to his amazement you begin to shout. He doesn't know it, but you heard a Word.

CONSIDERATIONS

1. "All too often people are so close to the devil that they are not intimidating his kingdom at all." Are you living too close to the kingdom of darkness?

   _____

2. The Holy Spirit is speaking words of truth, guidance, and strength. He speaks what He hears in Heaven. How attuned are you to hearing the Holy Spirit?

   _____

   _____

3. Hearing from the Holy Spirit causes you to lift your head toward Heaven. Make a conscious effort to lift your head and gaze into the heaven-lies when you are taking a walk; washing the

dishes, the kids, or the dog; getting into your car; before you go to bed; and when you wake up.

_____

4. Satan cannot tempt or attack you when you are hearing a Word from God through the Holy Spirit. What do you want God to destroy with His consuming fire?

_____

_____

_____

5. Read the full story of Elijah and the fifty men in Second Kings chapter 1 and write what that passage means to you.

_____

_____

_____

_____

MEDITATION

*So Elijah answered and said to the captain of fifty,
"If I am a man of God, then let fire come down from
Heaven and consume you and your fifty men." And
fire came down from Heaven and consumed him
and his fifty* (2 Kings 1:10).

God can and will send His fire from Heaven to consume
the kingdom of darkness. To those in the light of His presence, He will give peace.

DAY 38
LORD, HELP!

*But those who wait on the Lord shall **renew their***
__strength__… (Isaiah 40:31).

God says, "If you wait on Me, I'll renew your strength. If you wait on Me, everything will be all right."

You may be hurting right now, but be patient. Help is on the way.

I know you've cried out, "Lord, help! I've fallen, and I can't get up."

The Holy Spirit says, "Wait. Help is on the way. Just hold on, God is coming to your aid. He's coming to deliver you and to set you free."

God is going to bring you out and loose you from your captivity. He's going to renew your strength. If you hold on a little while longer, your change is going to come.

Remember Samson who lost everything; he lost his hair, his strength, and his eyes. Samson lost his position, his family, his wife, and his reputation. He was reduced from a great warrior to grinding at the mill. But without a doubt, at an appointed time, Samson's strength was renewed.

Samson's attitude was, "Lord, I'm waiting on you. If you don't help me, I'll die without ever being redeemed from the error of my ways. Lord, if you don't help me, I'll never get my honor back. God, if you don't help me, I'll never get up from where I've fallen."

While he was waiting, Samson's strength began to return.

The secret to renewing your strength is waiting on the Lord. God's Word says, *"But they that wait upon the Lord shall renew their strength…"* (Isaiah 40:31 KJV).

CONSIDERATIONS

1. God says, "If you wait on Me, I'll renew your strength. If you wait on Me, everything will be all right." Do you believe this? Have you had to wait for God to renew your strength? Write about that time.

   _____

   _____

   _____

2. Are you an impatient person? Think of ways you can keep yourself from becoming irritated while having to wait, such as counting your blessings.

   _____

   _____

   _____

3. Samson and Job had to wait on the Lord to renew their strength. List a few other biblical people or people you know who have had their strength renewed after waiting on the Lord.

_____

_____

_____

_____

_____

4. When you cry out to the Lord for help, are you willing to wait for His answer?

_____

5. Waiting and waiting patiently are two different things. Explain the difference.

_____

_____

_____

_____

MEDITATION

*But those who wait on the Lord shall **renew their strength**…* (Isaiah 40:31).

Determine to wait patiently for the Lord to renew your strength.

Day 39
As Gold

*But He knows the way that I take; when He has tested me, I shall come forth **as gold** (Job 23:10).*

Job endured tremendous emotional pain and physical affliction. His troubles were not only known to God but were allowed by God. Losing his sons and daughters and possessions left Job feeling very much alone. He looked at his situation from every possible angle trying to find God.

Every gold mine is hidden beneath the earth. Mining priceless jewels takes many hours of painstaking labor. Tons of earth must be removed to find the gold.

In the same way, a gold mine is buried beneath your flesh. Crucifying your flesh is excruciating, but it must occur to reveal the priceless jewels within you. Give God digging rights. After all, the mine belongs to Him. Allow Him to dig deeply and bring out buried treasure.

The devil knows you're a gold mine waiting to be claimed and mined. Your adversary has covered your priceless jewels with your past unconfessed sins, emotional traumas, and religious tradition. The devil knows that you have been buried alive. You merely need the Spirit to move, and the Word uncovers you. You are Heaven's best-kept secret and hell's worst nightmare.

We can attain a place in God that is higher than our problems, giving us a divine perspective. We must be led to this place. It is against our nature to want this rock. We must oppose our flesh and say, "When my spirit is overwhelmed, my spirit goes beyond nature and finds satisfaction only in the supernatural." We ask God to do something our flesh does not want: to lead us to the rock—Jesus—and away from earthly logic.

CONSIDERATIONS

1. "There is a gold mine buried beneath your flesh. Crucifying your flesh is excruciating, but it must occur to reveal the priceless jewels within you." What type of jewels do you imagine within you?

   _____

   _____

   _____

2. "Your enemy has covered your jewels with your past unconfessed sins, emotional traumas, and religious tradition." Do you know this is true?

   _____

   _____

   _____

3. When you give God digging rights, the mine belongs to Him. Will you allow Him to dig deeply and bring out your buried treasure?

_____

_____

_____

_____

4. When the Spirit moves and the Word uncovers you, you will become Heaven's best-kept secret and hell's worst nightmare. Allow the Spirit to move in you today.

_____

5. You can attain a place in God that is higher than your problems, giving you a divine, golden perspective. Have you reached this place yet?

_____

_____

_____

_____

MEDITATION

*But He knows the way that I take; when He has tested me, I shall come forth **as gold*** (Job 23:10).

Allow God to test you so that you will shine as gold in a world of darkness.

Day 40
The Spirit of the Lord

The Spirit of the Lord is upon Me, because He has anointed Me to preach the gospel to the poor; He has sent Me to heal the brokenhearted, to proclaim liberty to the captives and recovery of sight to the blind, to set at liberty those who are oppressed (Luke 4:18).

Approximately five out of ten marriages end in divorce. Those broken homes leave a trail of broken dreams, people, and children. Only the Master can heal these victims in the times in which we live. He can treat the long-term effects of this tragedy.

One of the great healing balms of the Holy Spirit is forgiveness. To forgive is to break the link between you and your past. Sadly enough, many times the person hardest to forgive is the one in the mirror. Although they rage loudly about others, people secretly blame themselves for a failed relationship.

Regardless of who you hold responsible, there is no healing in blame! When you begin to realize that your past does not necessarily dictate the outcome of your future, then you can release the hurt. It is impossible to inhale new air until you exhale the old.

I pray that as you continue reading, God would give the grace of releasing where you have been so you can receive what God has for you now.

Exhale, then inhale; there is more for you.

CONSIDERATIONS

1. Has your family been affected by divorce? Write the names of the people involved and pray to God for their emotional, spiritual, and mental restoration.

   _____

   _____

   _____

2. "One of the great healing balms of the Holy Spirit is forgiveness." Are there people you need to forgive who are in your present or past? Ask the Holy Spirit to help you forgive them.

   _____

   _____

   _____

3. "Many times the person hardest to forgive is the one in the mirror." Ask the Holy Spirit to reveal the deep roots within that keep you from forgiving yourself. Then give it to God and forgive yourself as He has forgiven you.

_____

_____

4. Your past does not necessarily have to dictate your future. Make a list of past hurts, abuses, failures, and sadnesses, then allow the Spirit of the Lord to give you peace and release from each one.

_____

_____

5. Exhale old, corrupted air and inhale new, fresh air to strengthen yourself for the journey into your God-given destiny.

_____

_____

MEDITATION

The Spirit of the Lord is upon Me, because He has anointed Me to preach the gospel to the poor; He has sent Me to heal the brokenhearted, to proclaim liberty to the captives and recovery of sight to the blind, to set at liberty those who are oppressed (Luke 4:18).

Do what you can to preach the Gospel to the poor, heal the brokenhearted, proclaim liberty to the captives, reveal Light to the blinded, and free the oppressed.

Day 41
Triplets

But the fruit of the Spirit is love, joy, peace, longsuf-
fering, kindness, goodness, faithfulness, gentleness,
self-control. Against such there is no law
(Galatians 5:22-23).

The atmosphere is your surroundings. You may find yourself in a very hostile atmosphere where the fruit and works of the flesh are being manifested. As you yield to the Holy Spirit, however, He will throw a wet blanket on the unkind thing that you wanted to say. The Holy Spirit will build a fire of His own that will bring warmth to a cold atmosphere, hope to a despairing atmosphere, joy to a saddening atmosphere, and love to a bitter, revengeful atmosphere. This is why the first three triplets—love, joy, and peace—are *atmosphere*-changing fruit.

The second three triplets—longsuffering, gentleness, goodness—are *attitude*-changing fruit. Even though we are saved and filled with the Holy Spirit, each of us has the potential to have an attitude. God sometimes lets us go through difficult situations to let us see what's really inside us. When we see our own helplessness, weaknesses, and despair, it causes us to cry out, "God, I need You!"

You have a strength that defies human logic. You have an ability to stand that you cannot attribute to anyone but God. You have a peace that even the apostle Paul couldn't understand, so he called it the *"peace of God, which passeth all understanding"* (Phil. 4:7 KJV). We call this third triplet—faith, meekness, and self-control—*attribute*-changing fruit because these qualities cannot be attributed to you but only to the Holy Spirit.

Within you lies the ability to become whatever you choose to be.

CONSIDERATIONS

1. The first three triplets—love, joy, and peace—
   are *atmosphere*-changing fruit. Describe how the
   first three triplets can change the atmosphere in
   your life.

   _____

   _____

2. The second three triplets—longsuffering, gentleness, and goodness—are *attitude*-changing fruit.
   Do you need an attitude adjustment? In what
   ways?

   _____

   _____

   _____

3. The third three triplets—faith, meekness, and self-control—are *attribute*-changing fruit, because these qualities cannot be attributed to you but only to the Holy Spirit. Are these three attributes working within you? Why or why not?

   _____

   _____

   _____

4. You have a strength within that defies human logic. Are you accessing that strength when troubles arise, or are you stumbling under the weight?

   _____

   _____

5. "Within you lies the ability to become whatever you choose to be." Do you believe this statement? Write what you want to become. Take steps toward achieving that goal.

   _____

   _____

MEDITATION

*But the fruit of the Spirit is love, joy, peace, longsuf-
fering, kindness, goodness, faithfulness, gentleness,
self-control. Against such there is no law*
(Galatians 5:22-23).

Plant a fruit tree in your spirit and watch it grow in love.

Day 42
Live by Faith

*I have been crucified with Christ; it is no longer I
who live, but Christ lives in me; and the life which I
now live in the flesh I **live by faith** in the Son of
God, who loved me and gave Himself for me*
(Galatians 2:20).

When a seed is dropped into the ground and
covered, it lies dormant for a season. No one
can see it; no one can tell that anything is
happening. But during this time the process of germination takes place. The casing is dying; the heart of grain is
sprouting.

In the spiritual realm it is no different. The apostle Paul
tells the Galatians:

257

Mortify therefore your members which are upon the earth; fornication, uncleanness, inordinate affection, evil concupiscence, and covetousness, which is idolatry (Colossians 3:5 KJV).

Mortify is a term related to mortuary, a place where we find nothing but dead and dysfunctional bodies.

What is Paul saying? Stop your Adamic nature from being the dominant force in your life. Allow the Holy Spirit to work in you, putting to death the flesh so that new life may sprout from you.

The storehouse of Heaven is full. You will never exhaust its inventory of glory. If we aren't walking in such a way to access it, however, these glorious realities will never occur in our lives.

Many Christians never access the windows of Heaven because they are still living in the outer court and have never broken through to the third dimension, the holy of holies. Many live in defeat and carnality because they have remained on the same level where they first boarded the ark of salvation.

CONSIDERATIONS

1. Have you allowed the Holy Spirit to put to death the flesh so that new life may sprout from you?

   _____

   _____

2. *"Mortify therefore your members…fornication, uncleanness, inordinate affection, evil concupiscence, and covetousness, which is idolatry"* (Col. 3:5 KJV). Staying away from evil is vital to living a life of faith. Have you turned away from all that is evil?

   _____

   _____

   _____

3. To access Heaven's storehouse of glory, you must obey God's Word. Are you doing your best to keep yourself pure and sin-free?

_____

_____

4. Are you still living in the outer court rather than moving toward and into the holy of holies where God showers His own with riches in glory?

_____

_____

5. Define what it means to you to live by faith.

_____

_____

_____

MEDITATION

*I have been crucified with Christ; it is no longer I
who live, but Christ lives in me; and the life which I
now live in the flesh I **live by faith** in the Son of
God, who loved me and gave Himself for me*
(Galatians 2:20).

Living by faith means believing that God is real, Jesus
died for your salvation, and you will live eternally with Him
in Heaven. Are you living by faith?

DAY 43
I KNOW THEM

*My sheep hear My voice, and **I know them**, and they follow Me* (John 10:27).

God says, "I know your name." God knows our name or reputation. God says, "Yes, I have heard the gossip. I have heard what kind of reputation you have." Did you know that God knows your name and still loves you?

God says, "I know the truth. I know your name." God knows that your name is Jacob but still asks, "What is your name?" Anytime an all-wise, all-knowing God asks a question, it isn't for His benefit. You need to confess, "My name is Jacob." Even though He knows our name, He wants us to confess it because He is going to change our name and speak a glorious destiny over us.

Within you are gifts, callings, and talents that have been weakened, pressed down, or held back. Your vision, dream, or desire may have been crushed. You may not have had any control over the circumstances. Perhaps your disobedience grieved the Holy Spirit. But arise, my friend! Whatever the devil did to you, he didn't complete the job. He left some strength in you.

Apostle Paul said: *"...Therefore most gladly I will rather boast in my infirmities, that the power of Christ may rest upon me"* (2 Cor. 12:9). When his strength had given out and his resources were exhausted, he had no other place to turn. He could rely on no other strength but the strength that God gave him.

Your own strength is not enough, but if you will take what's left of it and give it to God, who is more than enough, you will find Him to be sufficient.

CONSIDERATIONS

1. God says, "Yes, I have heard the gossip. I have heard what kind of reputation you have and I still love you." Can you say this about all the people you know?

   _____

   _____

   _____

2. "Within you are gifts, callings, and talents that have been weakened, pressed down, or held back." Knowing that Jesus loves you gives you strength to resurrect your gifts, callings, and talents. Do so today!

3. *"...Therefore most gladly I will rather boast in my infirmities, that the power of Christ may rest upon*

me" (2 Cor. 12:9). Like the apostle Paul, believers must glory in tough times so that the power of Christ will rest upon us. Is the power of Christ resting on you?

_____

_____

_____

_____

4. God knows your name. You know God's name. Call on His name when you are running out of strength. Write 10-12 names by which God is known, such as I Am, Good Shepherd, et cetera.

_____

_____

_____

_____

_____

_____

5. Your own strength is not enough, but if you take what's left and give it to God, He will multiply your strength over and over again.

_____

_____

MEDITATION

*My sheep hear My voice, and **I know them**, and they follow Me* (John 10:27).

Does Jesus know you?

DAY 44
STAND ON THE ROCK

*And the Lord said, "Here is a place by Me, and you shall **stand on the rock** (Exodus 33:21).*

The spirit is saved by faith, and the body is saved by hope. We must understand the working of the Holy Spirit in our lives. Many become discouraged when they fall short of their goals as a child of God. Others throw in the towel and say, "What's the use?"

Many of you are near a breakthrough in your life. You may have fought for years to get to where you are with God. Many of you are pregnant with destiny. You are carrying within the womb of your spirit a ministry that could change this world.

Remember, whenever God got ready to manifest Himself in glory and splendor, He always took the person up to a mountain or an elevated domain. Then He would manifest Himself.

Jesus is the Rock, and when we hide ourselves in Him we are taken to higher heights and deeper depths.

Some of you are going through a storm, a trial, or something you don't even understand. You're saying to yourself, "I've been faithful. I'm committed to my call. I've exercised my gift, but I still don't understand why this is happening to me."

Don't lose your focus. Help is on the way. What you face will be nothing more than a cleft in the rock. As you go through this problem, you will begin to understand the words of the old hymn, "Rock of Ages, cleft for me."

CONSIDERATIONS

1. "The spirit is saved by faith, and the body is saved by hope." Write what this concept means to you.

   _____

   _____

2. Many have become discouraged when they fell short of their goals as a child of God. Have you ever felt like throwing in the towel and saying, "What's the use?" Are you still saying that? Or have you moved forward in your walk of faith?

   _____

   _____

   _____

3. Are you "pregnant with destiny"? What do you need to do to birth a deeper relationship with God, a new business, a needed ministry, or a career change?

_____

_____

4. You may be going through a storm, a trial, or something you don't understand. Do you have the faith to believe that God is working all things for good for those who love Him?

_____

_____

5. You may think, "I've been faithful. I'm commit-ted to my call. I've exercised my gift, but I still don't understand why this is happening to me." Are your feet firmly planted on the Rock who will provide the answer in His perfect timing?

_____

_____

MEDITATION

*And the Lord said, "Here is a place by Me, and you shall **stand on the rock*** (Exodus 33:21).

Are you standing on the rock beside the Lord?

DAY 45
HOW YOU HAVE FALLEN

*How you are fallen from Heaven, O Lucifer, son of
the morning! How you are cut down to the ground,
you who weakened the nations! For you have said in
your heart: "I will ascend into Heaven, I will exalt
my throne above the stars of God; I will also sit on
the mount of the congregation on the farthest sides of
the north; I will ascend above the heights of the
clouds, I will be like the Most High"*
(Isaiah 14:12-14).

D riven by self-deception, prideful self-delusion, and self-importance, lucifer considered himself better than God. This explains why most of his statements begin with the word "I."

During the 1980s, several nationally-known televangelists let their fame and fortune get the best of them. As a result, pride prevented them from acknowledging their need of God. Considering themselves to be beyond reproach or advice, they let their guards down. Sin entered their lives, eventually destroying their ministries, their families, and their reputations.

When people (especially Christians who are not rooted and grounded in the Word) start acquiring prestige and experiencing monetary prosperity, they often forget that not long ago they had nothing.

In spite of their lack, they still managed to give God the glory whether it was by word of mouth or by giving in the offering. They knew that God would meet their needs. But once they came into a place of prosperity, they forgot it was God and God alone who blessed them. Now they look to their jobs or their businesses—or even their ministries—as their source. That is a dangerous place to be.

CONSIDERATIONS

1. Do you know people who are driven by self-deception, prideful self-delusion, and self-importance? How does God regard these people? Search Scripture for support.

   _____

   _____

   _____

2. If you remember the televangelists' scandals in the 1980s, write what you thought at the time. Write what you think now about the situations that occurred since.

   _____

   _____

3. Acquiring prestige and experiencing monetary prosperity can be ways that satan can tempt, attack, and destroy. How can you guard against him when success comes your way?

_____

_____

_____

4. Is it harder to be close to God when you are poor or wealthy? Why?

_____

_____

_____

5. Lucifer fell from Heaven because of his pride. Has pride made you stumble and fall? Describe the situation and vow to rid pride from your life.

_____

_____

_____

MEDITATION

How you are fallen from Heaven, O Lucifer, son of the morning! How you are cut down to the ground, you who weakened the nations! For you have said in your heart: "I will ascend into Heaven, I will exalt my throne above the stars of God; I will also sit on the mount of the congregation on the farthest sides of the north; I will ascend above the heights of the clouds, I will be like the Most High" (Isaiah 14:12-14).

Only the Most High can be the Most High. Don't aspire to be more than God created you to be.

DAY 46
BY WAY OF THE WILDERNESS

Then he said, "Which way shall we go up?" And he
*answered, "**By way of the Wilderness** of Edom"*
(2 Kings 3:8).

King Jehoshaphat asked the question, "How shall we go up against Moab to get victory?" The unexpected answer was, "You have to go through the wilderness of Edom to get the victory."

My friend, if you want to get the victory, you must be willing to go through the wilderness. I want to reiterate this fact: it is not always easy to get the victory because it belongs to the other side of the wilderness. You must be willing to go through a little time of abasement, confusion, adversity, and even opposition before you arrive at your destination.

Many may think that it is unfair to have to go through this phase. But you see, it is the wilderness that weeds out the saints from the "ain'ts." It is the wilderness that weeds out people who really want to do something for God from people who just have a momentary, superficial, mundane relationship with Him. It is the wilderness that makes a hypocrite back up and say, "I can't take it anymore." The wilderness, God's killing field, will weed out all the impostors because they cannot survive the adversity of the wilderness.

I want to warn you that you will have to go through the wilderness to attain the will of God for your life. The wilderness teaches you to stand; it teaches you to cast your cares upon Him. It teaches you to rely and totally depend on Him for life support, because you know in due season you shall reap if you faint not.

CONSIDERATIONS

1. You must be willing to go through the wilderness—
   a little time of abasement, confusion, adversity,
   and even opposition—before you arrive victoriously at your destination. Have you been wandering through the wilderness? Don't faint, keep
   moving forward.

   _____

   _____

2. The wilderness experience weeds out the saints
   from the "aint's." Which one are you?

   _____

   _____

3. "The wilderness, God's killing field, weeds out
   all the impostors because they cannot survive the

adversity of the wilderness." Describe a wilderness time in your life and tell how you survived.

_____

_____

_____

_____

_____

4. Wilderness times teach you to rely and totally depend on Him for life support. Is He your total life support system?

_____

_____

5. You will receive strength even in the wilderness as He provides nourishment and mercy.

MEDITATION

*Then he said, "Which way shall we go up?" And he
answered, "By way of the Wilderness of Edom"*
(2 Kings 3:8).

Know that you will walk *through* the wilderness to victory. Keep moving forward!

DAY 47
WHO CAN BE AGAINST US?

What then shall we say to these things? If God is for us, who can be against us? (Romans 8:31)

Some of us cannot handle the smallest problems. We feel that the hardships placed in our path indicate that God either has forsaken us or is punishing us for some sin we have committed. The devil has successfully employed that lie to deter us from seeking the heavenly Father. Do not for a moment think that you can do it on your own. You will fail woefully.

Remember Joshua and Caleb. Had they tried to enter the Promised Land on their own strength or cognizance, they would have perished in the wilderness. Even when life in the wilderness became dull and unappealing, they did not stop seeking God, neither did they cease to rely on His guidance.

Like Joshua and Caleb, we must be persistent in faith even in the wilderness where problems are at their peak.

The greatest battle that we face while we are in the wilderness is the one between the new and the old self. The old self that God is trying to kill in the wilderness refuses to die. It wants to resurrect old hurts and old problems. But, as new creatures in Christ Jesus, we must put the old self to death. Despite the situations you are facing, you must constantly remind yourself that you are a new creature and the old self is dead!

CONSIDERATIONS

1. You may feel that the hardships placed in your path indicate that God either has forsaken you or is punishing you for some sin you have committed. Know that this is satan's tactic to keep you from seeking God's presence.

2. When God is for you, you can stand firm with strength to win every battle. How confident are you that God can give you the victory?

   _____

   _____

   _____

   _____

3. Joshua and Caleb were mentioned as having faith through the wilderness. Write the names of

others who showed this kind of faith and strength, such as Joseph, Moses, and Paul.

_____

_____

_____

4. The greatest battle that you face while in the wilderness is the one between your new and old self. How hard is it for you to discard the old ways of the flesh and walk in with the Spirit?

_____

_____

5. The old self that God is trying to kill in the wilderness does not die easily. It wants to resurrect old hurts and old problems to keep you from the freedom that is yours in Christ. How much of your old self are you still dragging around with you?

_____

_____

MEDITATION

*What then shall we say to these things? If God is for us, **who can be against us?*** (Romans 8:31)

When wandering through the wilderness where satan is trying to devour you, remember that when God is for you it doesn't matter who is against you.

DAY 48
HIM ONLY

*And Jesus answered and said to him, "Get behind Me, Satan! For it is written, 'You shall worship the Lord your God, and **Him only** you shall serve'"* (Luke 4:8).

My God is the Alpha and the Omega, the Beginning and the End. There is nothing too hard for Him. There is nothing He cannot handle. Because we know who we are in Christ Jesus and what we mean to our heavenly Father, satan tries to discourage us. He tries to use sickness, financial problems, family stress, and anything and everything you can think of to incapacitate us. The question you must ask yourself is, "Who is my God? Whom do I serve?" Then answer the question with, "My God is the Way-Maker." Remember, if God be for us, who can be against us?

God is so real in my inward man. He has not only washed away all my sins, but He has filled my cup with His love so that my cup bubbles over. He is the Lover of my soul; He is the Answer to my every need; He is my Burden-Bearer. Maybe you are the kind of person who can handle everything that comes your way, but I can't. However, I know someone who is able to take it. His name is Jesus Christ.

The enemy fights those who know who they are and whose they are. The Bible affirms that God is faithful (see 1 Cor. 1:9). The Word of God states:

But to us there is but one God, the Father, of whom are all things, and we in Him; and one Lord Jesus Christ, by whom are all things, and we by Him (1 Corinthians 8:6 KJV).

CONSIDERATIONS

1. Because you know who you are in Christ Jesus and what you mean to your heavenly Father, satan tries to discourage you. He uses sickness, financial problems, family stress, anything and everything to incapacitate you. What are three ways to keep from becoming discouraged?

   _____

   _____

   _____

   _____

2. There is nothing too hard for God to handle. God loves you more than satan hates you. Believing Him only will strengthen you moment by moment.

3. God has not only washed away all your sins, but He has filled your cup so full with His love that it bubbles over. Thank Him only for your salvation and eternal joy.

4. *"God is faithful, by whom you were called into the fellowship of His Son, Jesus Christ our Lord"* (1 Cor. 1:9). God wants us to fellowship with His only begotten Son, Jesus. This is an amazing honor for believers.

5. *"But to us there is but **one God**, the Father, of whom are all things, and we in Him; and **one Lord Jesus Christ**, by whom are all things, and we by Him"* (1 Cor. 8:6 KJV). Write what this verse means to you.

_____

_____

_____

_____

MEDITATION

*And Jesus answered and said to him, "Get behind
Me, Satan! For it is written, 'You shall worship the
Lord your God, and **Him only** you shall serve'"*
(Luke 4:8).

Are you serving more than one "god"? Think about it.

DAY 49
ASK GOD

*If any of you lacks wisdom, let him **ask of God**, who gives to all liberally and without reproach, and it will be given to him (James 1:5).*

I was taught not to ask God, "Why?" I was taught that true Christians never ask God why. It was considered a breach of our faith to ask God why. If you really believe God, you just completely accept everything that comes your way without asking God anything pertaining to its reason for happening. It's as if God gets insulted, mad, or feels like you're questioning His authority when you ask Him why. Others feel that if you ask why God is intimidated with your quest for knowledge, or they worry that you might ask Him something that He cannot answer, or they fear that you might offend or hinder God's ability to be omniscient. For whatever the reason, you just don't ask Almighty God, "Why?"

However, the Bible says, *"If any of you lack wisdom, let him ask of God, that giveth to all men liberally, and upbraideth not…"* (James 1:5 KJV). God said, "Come to Me and ask Me why." He said, "I'm not afraid of your questions. I'm not afraid of you." God is not insecure in His sovereignty. He's not envious of humans or afraid that His position, power, or authority is going to be jeopardized by you or anybody else knowing too much. I don't care how many times you have to ask Him.

God says He can handle it. Bring it to Him. "I'm able," says God, "to share with you the kind of truth that transforms." God says, "Cry out to Me; inquire of Me. Knock and the door shall be opened, seek and you shall find."

CONSIDERATIONS

1. "I was taught that true Christians never ask God why. It was considered a breach of our faith to ask God why." Is this the way you were raised? Do you believe this is the correct approach to living according to God's will?

   _____

   _____

2. "If you really believe God, you just completely accept everything that comes your way without asking God anything pertaining to its reason for happening." Many Christians feel this way. Do you? Why or why not?

   _____

   _____

3. Have you ever wanted to ask God why but were afraid? Were you afraid of His answer or your motivations?

_____

_____

_____

_____

4. Did you ever ask God a question and you thought He didn't answer? Are you still waiting for that answer, or did you reconsider the question?

_____

_____

_____

_____

5. Asking God allows Him to share His truth—the Truth—with you. Ask, seek, knock.

MEDITATION

*If any of you lacks wisdom, let him **ask of God**, who gives to all liberally and without reproach, and it will be given to him* (James 1:5).

No matter your IQ, ask God for wisdom and then use that wisdom to fulfill your destiny.

DAY 50
REACHING FORWARD

Brethren, I do not count myself to have apprehended;
but one thing I do, forgetting those things which are
*behind and **reaching forward** to those things which*
are ahead, I press toward the goal for the prize of the
upward call of God in Christ Jesus
(Philippians 3:13-14).

M y brothers and sisters, you must continue to obey and serve God. You are going to show your critics and the unbelievers that you, as the servant of God, will win in the end. Some critics will bet against you and they will speak against you. They will say, "That girl ain't never gonna be nothing. Her mama was nothing. Her aunt was nothing. I knew her grandmother and she was nothing. Her granddaddy was nothing. Her father was nothing, and she's gonna be nothing."

According to the Word of God, *"Therefore, if anyone is in Christ, he is a new creation; old things have passed away; behold, all things have become new"* (2 Cor. 5:17). God said that we are going to make a liar out of all of them.

Stop believing those lying prophecies of the past. Stop believing people and teachers who called you stupid. Turn a deaf ear to racism and sexism. Become renewed to the truth of God. You might have had a bad childhood, and you might have been abused, misused, rejected, and neglected. God says forget those things that are behind you and reach forward.

When God speaks a word into our lives, as far as He is concerned it has already been accomplished.

CONSIDERATIONS

1. You must continue to obey and serve God. You must show your critics and unbelievers that you, as the servant of God, will win in the end. Write about what discourages you the most. Then give that issue to God and walk ahead with strength and courage.

   _____

   _____

   _____

2. Do you believe people when they criticize or belittle you? Remember that you are God's creation. He made you special and unique. Be strengthened in His love.

   _____

3. Remember back to when someone said something that left a scar on your heart and in your mind. Write that experience on a piece of paper; now ask God to help you forgive that person, ask Him to erase that scar, and then tear up that paper and toss it into the garbage.

4. "...*forgetting those things which are behind* and *reaching forward to those things which are ahead*" is what you must do to claim victory for today and all your tomorrows.

5. Are you "pressing toward the goal for the prize of the upward call of God in Christ Jesus"? When you are you will receive strength to keep moving forward toward Him and your God-given destiny.

_____

_____

MEDITATION

*Brethren, I do not count myself to have apprehended;
but one thing I do, forgetting those things which
are behind and **reaching forward** to those things
which are ahead, I press toward the goal for the
prize of the upward call of God in Christ Jesus*
(Philippians 3:13-14).

Are you reaching forward and pressing toward the goal?

Reflections

_____

_____

_____

_____

_____

_____

_____

_____

_____

_____

_____

_____

_____

_____

_____

_____

_____

_____

_____

_____

_____

_____

_____

_____

_____

_____

_____

_____

_____

_____

_____

_____

_____

_____

_____

_____

_____

_____

_____

_____

_____

_____

_____

_____

_____

_____

_____

_____

_____

_____

_____

_____

_____

_____

_____

_____

_____

_____

_____

_____

_____

_____

_____

_____

_____

_____

_____

_____

_____

_____

_____

_____

_____

_____

_____

_____

_____

_____

_____

_____

_____

_____

_____

_____

_____

_____

_____

_____

_____

_____

_____

_____

_____

_____

_____

_____

_____

_____

_____

_____

_____

_____

_____

_____

_____

_____

_____

_____

_____

_____

_____

_____

_____

_____

_____

_____

_____

_____

_____

_____

_____

_____

_____

_____

_____

_____

_____

_____

_____

_____

_____

_____

_____

_____

_____

_____

_____

_____

_____

_____

_____

_____

_____

_____

_____

_____

_____

_____

_____

SOW THIS BOOK INTO SOMEONE'S LIFE

Don't let the impact of this book end with you!
Call us today and get a discount when you order 3 or more
books to sow into someone else's life.

1-888-987-7033

GET A FREE E-BOOK EVERY WEEK!

www.LifeSupernatural.com

Find spirit-filled resources and news for your
everyday life, PLUS sign up to find out about Free,
$.99 and $1.99 e-books each and every week!

Exclusive interviews with your favorite authors only at:

www.LifeSupernatural.com/podcast

Tune in today!

facebook.com/DestinyImage • twitter.com/DestinyImage